RAW FOOD

CELEBRATIONS

PARTY MENUS FOR EVERY OCCASION!

by

Nomi Shannon and Sheryl Duruz

books
Alive

Summertown, Tennessee

Library of Congress Cataloging-in-Publication Data

Shannon, Nomi.
   Raw food celebrations: party menus for every occasion / by
Nomi Shannon and Sheryl Duruz.
        p.   cm.
   Includes index.
   ISBN 978-1-57067-228-6
   1. Cookery (Natural foods)   2. Raw foods.   3. Menus.
4. Entertaining.   I. Duruz, Sheryl.   II. Title.

TX741.S5327 2008
641.5'636—dc22

                                        2008022229

Cover and interior design: *Aerocraft Charter Art Service*
Cover and interior photos: *Piers Duruz*

Printed in Canada

Books Alive
an imprint of Book Publishing Company
P.O. Box 99
Summertown, TN 38483
888-260-8458
www.bookpubco.com

ISBN 13: 978-1-57067-228-6

17 16 15 14 13 12 11 10 09 08   1 2 3 4 5 6 7 8 9

Book Publishing Co. is a member of Green
Press Initiative. We chose to print this title on
paper with postconsumer recycled content,
processed without chlorine, which saved the
following natural resources:

59 trees

2,772 pounds of solid waste

21,587 gallons of water

5,201 pounds of greenhouse gases

41 million BTU of total energy

For more information, visit
www.greenpressinitiative.org.

*Paper calculations from Environmental Defense
Paper Calculator, www.papercalculator.org*

CONTENTS

DEDICATIONS

from Nomi

To Seth Shannon Taylor.
I am so grateful to know you.

from Sheryl

To my husband Piers,
and our continuing adventures in life together.
You inspire me daily and I am so grateful to have you in my life.-

FOREWORD

When I picked up Nomi Shannon's first book, *The Raw Gourmet*, several years ago, I was immediately struck by the beauty and simplicity of it. Folded among the pages of astonishingly beautiful photographs of raw food creations were unexpectedly short, simple-to-follow, and yet rewarding recipes that used only a few basic ingredients to achieve spectacular results. I was hooked. That book still stands on my shelf as one of the milestone contributions to the world of raw food cuisine.

Now, it seems Nomi has achieved the remarkable yet again, this time teaming up with Sheryl Duruz and taking us on a whirlwind tour through rich cultural food traditions and tongue-teasing tastes while somehow managing to achieve a rare balance of artfulness and simplicity at the same time. The recipes in this book, *Raw Food Celebrations*, have become some of my instant favorites. Through Nomi's and Sheryl's guidance, these recipes will inspire you, humble you, and reward you with sheer delight as you munch, crunch, and lunch your way from one recipe to the next, treating yourself to the most healthful meals in the world while impressing friends and family with your newfound brilliance for creating genuine cuisine.

I'll admit I'm a crude preparer of nutritious foods. Most of what I gulp down from my morning blended superfood smoothie ritual is neither elegant nor attractive (blended sprouts and spirulina, after all, are not exactly appealing to the eye), but one afternoon, after using just three recipes from this book you're now holding, I managed to present a raw cuisine spread for family and friends that had them wondering if my body had been secretly switched with a clone who trained at an exotic culinary institute in some far-off land. Needless to say, they were impressed, and I was thrilled!

Whether you're looking to dive into a grand expression of raw food artfulness or simply fill your eager tummy with the most beautiful and nutritious foods in the world, *Raw Food Celebrations* may be just the book you're looking for. Nomi's and Sheryl's guidance provides exactly the direction you need to go from being a raw food novice like me to a true raw food artist respected by friends and family alike. I encourage you to dive right in, turn a few pages, get your hands drenched in lemon juice, and start discovering just how much fun it really is to eat the most healthful foods in the world!

Mike Adams

THE HEALTH RANGER, EDITOR OF NATURALNEWS.COM

INTRODUCTION

Nomi Shannon, raw food author, chef, and teacher from the United States, and Sheryl Duruz, raw food chef and teacher from Canada and Australia, teamed up across the continents to bring you *Raw Food Celebrations: Live Food Entertaining Made Easy.* The outcome of our exciting collaboration is a unique compilation of menus, recipes, full-color photographs, and plan-ahead guides designed to make your entertaining foolproof and fun. Use the menus as they are presented, or mix and match them as you like to create your own eclectic bill of fare.

Our objective with *Raw Food Celebrations* is to help you enjoy entertaining in your home with ease. We have created menus that range from the traditional to the exotic, including brunch, luncheon, and cocktail party ideas. You will be able to select either innovative or time-honored flavors to serve your guests. Whether or not your guests have an interest in nutritious raw cuisine, they are sure to enjoy the food and festivities.

We believe this is the first book of its kind, devoted exclusively to healthful raw menus and recipes designed for entertaining. To help you plan ahead, we've ensured that many of the recipes can be prepared in advance, leaving you time to decorate your table and relax a bit before company arrives so you can be the finest host possible.

Whether you are planning a graduation party, wedding shower, birthday celebration, or holiday gathering, we sincerely hope that *Raw Food Celebrations* becomes the guide you rely on year after year for all your happy occasions.

Nomi and Sheryl

RAW FOOD

CELEBRATIONS

PARTY MENUS FOR EVERY OCCASION!

TIPS FOR A SUCCESSFUL EVENT

A great celebration is the culmination of meticulous planning, advance preparation, and the ability to harmonize many diverse factors, including the right balance of people, food, theme, and decor. You can ensure a successful celebration by doing the hard work prior to your gathering and providing a positive, fun experience for all of your guests. Here are some tips that will help you to foolproof your event.

■ **Get organized.** Several weeks or even months before your event, determine the type of get-together you want to have (buffet, sit-down meal, or cocktail party) and the size. Compile your guest list and make sure you have a compatible group of people who will enjoy each other's company and keep the conversation rolling. A balanced mix of people will keep your party lively.

■ **Finalize your menu a few weeks in advance.** This will give you plenty of time to track down hard-to-find ingredients, purchase or borrow essential equipment you don't already own, and make any necessary menu revisions without waiting until the last minute.

■ **Arrange a trial run of the menu.** If at all possible, give the recipes a test drive before the big day. Invite a few of your friends, family members, or volunteer helpers to taste-test all of the dishes. A trial run will give you a chance to work out any glitches, avoid unpleasant surprises, and see how the meal pulls together before you are under pressure.

■ **Set aside time to clean your house, either before or after the bulk of the food is prepared.** A fresh house is inviting and will make your guests feel welcome.

■ **Decorate your home in accordance with the theme of your menu.** Even if your theme is simply a celebration of the season, include fresh flowers and other seasonal embellishments as part of your table setting, as plate and platter garnishes (edible flowers are especially attractive and make good points for conversation), and as adornments throughout your home.

■ **Prepare as many dishes (or parts of dishes) in advance as possible.** Some recipes can be made several days to a week or more prior to your event. Take advantage of the relaxed scheduling benefits this advance preparation affords; you'll be glad you did when the date of your event draws near.

■ **Don't underestimate the value of assistance.** If you have friends or family members who are adept at food preparation and enjoy it, even if they are unfamiliar with raw cuisine, enlist their help. Extra hands are always welcome for preparing complex or time-consuming dishes, laying out the buffet, refreshing drinks and refilling bowls or platters after guests arrive, or providing tableside service. If you are planning a large gathering or very involved menu, consider hiring one or two people who specialize in this type of assistance.

■ **Don't forget to arrange for the after-party cleanup.** Allow your guests to enjoy their time at your event without having to do any work. If they see or sense that you need help cleaning up afterward, they will feel obligated to pitch in. Instead, make sure you have arranged for some friends, family, or paid help (if you need it) to assist you with clearing tables, storing leftovers, washing dishes, sweeping up, and getting your house back in order. If you have all aspects of your event—from guest list to shopping to food prep to cleanup—sorted out in advance, everyone will enjoy your special gathering, including you.

The following equipment will allow you to create all of the recipes and menus in this book as well as raw food recipes from other sources. Although not all of these items are essential, they can be very helpful. Your initial investment in these high-quality tools will be well rewarded with years of reliable service, versatility in food preparation, and beautiful, impressive presentations.

CITRUS JUICER OR REAMER. A citrus juicer is an electric or manual device used to extract the juice from lemons, limes, oranges, and even grapefruits. It has a ridged cone onto which a halved fruit is pressed. A citrus reamer is a ridged, teardrop-shaped tool, often made of wood, with a handle.

DEHYDRATOR. A dehydrator is an electrical appliance that removes the natural moisture from food by slowly drying it at a low temperature. We prefer the Excalibur brand nine-tray model because it is the most flexible size, the temperature can be easily controlled, its almost-square shape is easier to work with than typical round dehydrators, and the air flow is superior to other brands. With a dehydrator, you can dry a wide range of fruits and vegetables, and because dried fruits store well at room temperature, you will find that it is convenient to keep a good supply of these dried foods on hand. A dehydrator will also expand your raw food repertoire by giving you the ability to make vegan raw cookies, crackers, nut loaves, snack bars, fruit leathers, sweet potato chips, burgers, and much more. For many recipes that require a dehydrator you will also need ParaFlexx Premium sheets. (ParaFlexx Premium sheets are available from suppliers that carry dehydrators. See Resources, page 103.) These

How Much Time Is Needed to Fully Dehydrate Foods?

The amount of time needed to fully dehydrate foods varies considerably and is dependent on the moisture content of the food, the humidity on the day you are dehydrating, and the thickness of the slices you are drying. As a general rule, allow 18 to 36 hours to fully dehydrate most foods, although some foods will take less time than this and some will take longer. Since fully dehydrated food will keep indefinitely, you can prepare it as far in advance as you would like. It's a good idea to begin the dehydrating process at least 72 hours before you want to use the item, just to be on the safe side.

The best way to be sure that food is fully dehydrated is to test it. To do this, allow the slices to cool to room temperature; then break open a few slices. They should be fairly brittle and completely dry all the way through, with no evidence of moisture. If you are unsure, simply continue dehydrating them for another 12 hours or so. Food that isn't fully dehydrated will get moldy within a few days, so it's worth taking additional care and time to ensure the food you are dehydrating is completely dry.

are commonly used for dehydrating foods that contain a lot of liquid, which would drip through the mesh sheets, or are very sticky. ParaFlexx Premium sheets are nonstick, washable, and reusable.

FOOD PROCESSOR. A food processor is an appliance used for chopping, slicing, grating, and shredding fruits and vegetables. With its curved blade (called an S blade), it is also useful for grinding nuts and puréeing pâtés and other mixtures that are too dry or thick to process in a blender.

HEAVY-DUTY JUICER. A heavy-duty juicer refers to a masticating or twin-gear juicer that not only makes juice, it also grinds and extrudes food with the use of a blank screen. Some brands we recommend are Champion, Green Power, and Green Star. Centrifugal juicers (ones that have a basket that must be removed and cleaned) are not the same as heavy-duty juicers and cannot perform the same functions.

HIGH-PERFORMANCE BLENDER. Ordinary blenders designed for home use have limited power and cannot accomplish the tasks that a high-performance blender can do with ease, such as purée frozen bananas and process thick mixtures. We recommend the Vita-Mix or the K-Tec HP3A Blender by Blendtec. If you do not have access to a high-performance blender, be sure to grate harder items like carrots or parsnips prior to blending them, and either avoid using frozen ingredients or partially defrost and finely chop them before adding them to the blender. You will also need to process mixtures longer in a regular home blender than you would need to with a high-performance blender.

ICE CREAM MAKER. There are two basic styles of ice cream makers—manual and electric—ranging from simple and inexpensive to fancy and high-end. Both styles are designed to freeze and aerate mixtures to create smooth frozen treats that are free of ice crystals.

MANDOLINE. A mandoline is a hand-operated tool that produces thick to ultrathin slices and julienne (matchsticks). It is especially useful when making large quantities of food or when having perfectly uniform pieces is important.

NUT MILK BAG. Also known as a sprout bag, a nut milk bag is a handy, washable, fine-mesh nylon bag. It is used to quickly strain out the ground nut pulp from homemade nut milks. It can also be used for growing sprouts from small seeds, such as broccoli, clover, and radish.

RAMEKIN. Typically small, round, and made of ceramic, a ramekin is a dish used for individual servings. The capacity of most ramekins ranges from four to six ounces.

SPIRAL SLICER. Also called a spiralizer, a spiral slicer creates long, thin, spaghetti-like strands from vegetables. Although zucchini is a favorite to "spiralize," a spiral slicer will work with most hard vegetables, such as beets, carrots, parsnips, sweet potatoes, and yams. Some popular brands are Saladacco and Spirooli. If you do not have a spiral slicer, you can use a vegetable peeler to make long, thin strands similar to linguine.

SPRINGFORM PAN. A springform pan is a metal cake pan with removable sides. Using this type of pan will help you make beautiful raw cakes with ease.

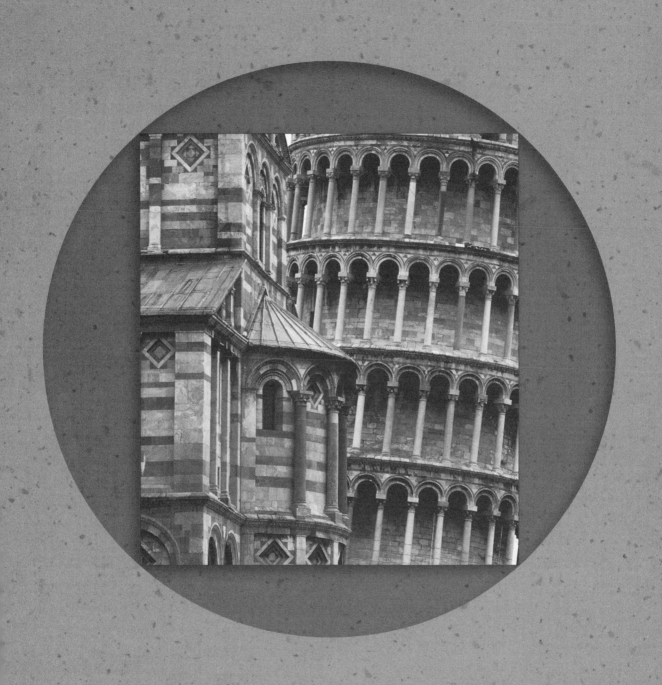

ITALIAN

Italian Menu

Menu

Greens with Lemon-Basil Dressing

Parsnip-Avocado Soup with Dehydrated Pepper Rounds

Zuochini Pasta with Pesto and Marinara Sauce

Creamy Tomato Lasagne

Chocolate-Caramel Divine Cheesecake or Lemon Gelato

Equipment Needed

blender

citrus juicer or reamer

dehydrator (optional)

food processor

mandoline (optional)

nut milk bag or fine-mesh strainer

spiral slicer or vegetable peeler

There is a secret to this meal. If you look carefully at the foods used, you will notice that despite this being a generously portioned meal with several distinct courses, the main ingredients are similar. There are a lot of tomatoes and zucchini, a fairly small quantity of nuts (in the white sauce for the lasagne), and very small amounts of oil, along with some greens and seasonings. Using the same ingredients in different ways minimizes the chance of indigestion from various combinations of foods. No one will ever notice your clever secret; your guests will just feel great after the meal.

Following the guidelines for serving quantities and postponing dessert for as long as possible after the main meal will help ensure that you and your guests will not suffer from "food coma," a sleepy feeling caused by overeating and poor food combining. A minimum of two hours between the meal and dessert is ideal. This delay will give everyone an opportunity to digest the main course before the sweets are presented.

Several weeks to several days before your event:

- dehydrate the pepper rounds for the soup garnish (see page 13)
- make Chocolate-Caramel Divine Cheesecake (page 24) and store it in the freezer

Three to four days before your event:

- do all of your grocery shopping
- store the zucchini and tomatoes at room temperature (they will keep longer and will taste better)

Two to three days before your event:

- make the four sauce recipes for the lasagne: White Sauce (page 19), Green Herb Sauce (page 19), Red Sauce (page 21), and Creamy Tomato Sauce (page 20)

One to two days before your event:

- prepare Zucchini Noodles (page 22)

Serving Suggestions

For a buffet, use your prettiest bowl or platter to serve the salad. If there is room on the buffet, use two sets of serving implements; this will make the line move more efficiently.

If this Italian menu will be a sit-down meal, we suggest that you serve the salad and soup courses in small portions. After all, there is still the main course to come—not to mention dessert! By serving the first courses on small plates, you will be doing your guests a big favor. For fun, trying serving the salad on small bread plates or in dessert bowls and the soup in teacups.

One day before your event:

- assemble the lasagne (page 18)
- make Pesto Sauce (page 15)
- make Marinara Sauce (page 16)
- make Lemon Gelato (page 25)
- wash and dry the salad greens (page 12)
- set out serving dishes, flatware, and table-cloths

The day of your event:

- make Parsnip-Avocado Soup (page 13)
- make Zucchini Pasta (page 14) and add the prepared Pesto Sauce
- toss the salad (page 12) just before serving

Add Surprising Taste and Color to Salads

When serving guests, the secret to a great salad is to have at least one or, even better, two surprise ingredients. For example, very thinly sliced fennel adds a pleasing taste surprise to a salad that is part of an Italian-themed meal. An excellent visual surprise is a sprinkling of pomegranate seeds on the salad and around the edge of the plate; they look like little, sparkling rubies. Another idea is to sprinkle raw sunflower seeds and very finely diced red bell pepper over the salad and around the edge of the plate. Alternatively, use almonds and orange sections or walnuts and grapefruit sections. Imagine star fruit, also called carambola, thinly sliced and scattered over the top of a salad. The fruit's striking star shape and lovely yellow color add eye appeal, and the ripe flesh adds a burst of refreshing, exotic flavor. When shopping for star fruit, remember that the best-tasting ones will be the most fragrant. Edible flowers are another eye-catching decoration. You might be surprised to know how many flowers are edible. The visual effects and fun of sampling rose, pansy, violet, or nasturtium flowers are unsurpassed. Think outside the box when selecting your surprise ingredients. Often a walk through the produce section of your grocery store will offer up exciting ideas.

An important rule for a great salad is to make sure that all the components are completely dry before the dressing is added. No dressing will taste right or have the proper consistency if it is tossed with wet greens. A salad spinner or large, clean towels are a must to ensure that your salad ingredients are dry.

In addition to fresh lettuce greens, consider adding other fresh green foods to your salads, such as asparagus, green beans, sugar snap peas, and sprouts; they will add interest and variety. Always include some colorful vegetables too, such as red, yellow, or orange bell peppers, carrots, or tomatoes. Make a simple dressing, toss it well with the lettuce and other vegetables, and then top off the salad with your two surprise ingredients.

Greens with Lemon-Basil Dressing

Preparation time: 10 minutes

Yield: 8 to 10 servings

The simplest of all salads will go best with this meal. Use a mix of baby greens, known as mesclun or spring mix, or tear up your favorite homegrown lettuce. Any dark green lettuce will work well. Plan on at least one cup of greens per person before the dressing has been added, and toss the dressing into the greens just moments before the meal is served. Add your two surprise elements (see sidebar, page 11) and your salad will be ready to go!

10 to 20 cups salad greens of your choice

¼ cup flaxseed oil

¼ cup freshly squeezed lemon juice

1 teaspoon Nama Shoyu, or a pinch of sea salt or seasoned salt

1 teaspoon dulse flakes

½ to 1 teaspoon agave syrup or maple syrup

2 fresh basil leaves, chopped, or ½ teaspoon dried basil

¼ teaspoon Italian seasoning

¼ teaspoon cayenne (optional)

▶ Sprinkle all of the ingredients over the salad greens and toss well.

VARIATION: Replace the lemon juice with ¼ cup balsamic vinegar.

Parsnip-Avocado Soup
WITH DEHYDRATED PEPPER ROUNDS

Preparation time: 20 minutes (plus advance time to dehydrate the pepper rounds)   **Yield:** 8 to 10 servings

This smooth, soothing soup is the perfect complement for a meal that has many strong flavors. It is a great middle course and palate cleanser. Serve very small portions so your guests won't be uncomfortably full and will have room for the remainder of the meal. This soup tastes best when it is served the same day it is made.

2 cups water

4 large parsnips

4 large stalks celery, peeled

1 ripe avocado

2 tablespoons plus 2 teaspoons flaxseed oil

2 teaspoons freshly squeezed lemon juice

2 teaspoons sea salt

16 to 20 dehydrated pepper rounds (see below)

▶ Combine the water, parsnips, celery, avocado, oil, lemon juice, and salt in a blender and process until smooth. Pour into serving bowls and garnish with the dehydrated pepper rounds.

VARIATION: Omit the dehydrated pepper rounds and garnish the soup with a sprig of fresh dill, fennel fronds, or finely diced red and yellow bell peppers.

NOTE: If you are using a regular home blender, grate the parsnips and cut the celery into small pieces prior to blending. Process the mixture as long as necessary to achieve a smooth consistency.

Dehydrated Pepper Rounds

Dehydrated pepper rounds can be made several weeks before your event. Thinly slice red, yellow, or orange bell peppers into rounds. Discard the stem and seeds. Dehydrate the rounds at 105 to 115 degrees F for 18 to 36 hours, or until they are totally dry and brittle (see sidebar, page 3). Allow them to cool completely, then store them in a tightly sealed jar or zipper-lock plastic bag at room temperature. Dehydrated pepper rounds will keep indefinitely. A garnish of one or two brightly colored pepper rounds floating on a bowl of soup or topping a salad is lovely and delicious. Fill your dehydrator with the pepper rounds, as you will find many uses for them.

NOTE: Use only red, yellow, or orange peppers and avoid the green ones; green peppers are not ripe and can cause digestive discomfort.

13

Zucchini Pasta with Pesto and Marinara Sauce

See photo between pages 22 and 23. **Yield:** 14 to 16 servings as a side dish; 8 to 10 servings as a main course

For Zucchini Pasta with Pesto and Marinara Sauce, first make the pesto. Why? Because once the zucchini has been spiralized it will start to weep. To prevent this, pour the pesto immediately over the zucchini as soon as it has been cut into noodles. Toss the zucchini with chop sticks or tongs until the pesto has completely coated each strand; this will seal in the juices from the zucchini and keep it from getting watery. Then make the marinara sauce. There is no need to wash the blender between the making the two sauces, as both recipes use several of the same ingredients.

When serving, never mix the marinara sauce with the zucchini pasta and pesto because red marinara and green pesto combine to make an unappetizing color. Place the marinara sauce on top of the pasta and pesto, either in a serving bowl if you are having a buffet, or on a dinner plate if you are having a sit-down meal. For a finishing touch, decorate each plate with a basil leaf or two and a cherry tomato.

ZUCCHINI PASTA

Preparation time: 5 to 10 minutes

To calculate how much zucchini you will need, allot half a medium zucchini per person when serving the pasta as a side dish and one medium zucchini per person when it will be the main course. Leftover Zucchini Pasta with Pesto will keep for a day or two in a tightly covered container in the refrigerator, but it is best served to company the day it is made. It is fine to prepare it a few hours in advance as long as you remember to immediately toss the pesto with the zucchini as soon as it has been spiralized.

8 to 10 medium-size zucchini

▶ **FOR THE PASTA,** cut the zucchini into thin noodles using a spiral slicer.

PESTO

See photo between pages 22 and 23. **Preparation time:** 10 minutes

FOR A SIDE DISH

6 tablespoons extra-virgin olive oil

2 tablespoons raw pine nuts

3 cloves garlic

1 tablespoon chopped fresh parsley

10 to 12 fresh basil leaves

Pinch of sea salt

FOR A MAIN COURSE

¾ cup extra-virgin olive oil

4 tablespoons raw pine nuts

6 cloves garlic

¾ cup fresh basil leaves, packed

2 tablespoons chopped fresh parsley

¼ teaspoon sea salt

Traditional pesto contains Parmesan cheese, olive oil, pine nuts, and basil. This flavor-packed recipe is similar to many traditional recipes minus the cheese. It can be made several hours to a day in advance. Store it in a covered container in the refrigerator.

▶ **FOR THE PESTO,** combine all of the ingredients in a blender and process until completely smooth. If the sauce is too thick, add 1 to 2 teaspoons of warm water until the desired consistency is achieved.

NOTE: If you are making the Marinara Sauce (page 16) immediately after the Pesto, don't wash your blender. The garlic and basil from the Pesto will add extra flavor to the Marinara Sauce.

MARINARA SAUCE

See photo between pages 22 and 23.   **Preparation time:** 25 minutes (plus advance soaking time)

Cooked marinara sauce, also known as Italian red sauce, gets its great flavor from simmering for a long time on the stove. The steam rising from the pot is the moisture being released, which reduces and thickens the sauce. In raw cuisine, there is a secret to creating a thick, rich, flavorful marinara sauce without cooking: dehydrated tomatoes (use only the dry tomatoes, not the ones packed in oil).

Experienced Italian cooks know that, in addition to long simmering, a fabulous red sauce often requires a little sweetener to offset the acidity of the tomatoes. If your sauce needs a bit of sweetening, blend in one or two soft dates at the end of the preparation.

This recipe is a general description. Prepare it the way most great chefs approach a recipe—season it lightly, then adjust the ingredients to suit your taste. Part of the magic of raw sauces is that they are very adaptable. We start with modest quantities and let you take it from there by tasting and seasoning as you go. Feel free to add whatever other ingredients you like in your red sauce, such as chopped olives.

It's not necessary to peel or seed the tomatoes. Buy extra tomatoes; that way, if you want to make more sauce, you will have everything you need on hand.

Dehydrating Tomatoes at Home

If you prefer, replace store-bought sun-dried tomatoes in recipes with your own dehydrated ones. Once you make your own dehydrated tomatoes, you'll never want to use store-bought ones again.

Thinly slice perfectly ripe tomatoes and arrange them on ParaFlexx Premium sheets so they don't drip through the mesh liners and make a mess. Dehydrate them at 105 to 115 degrees F for 10 to 20 hours. When they are dry to the touch on the top, place a dehydrator tray with a mesh liner (not a ParaFlexx sheet) on top, flip the two trays over together, lift the top tray, peel the ParaFlexx sheet off the tomatoes, if necessary, and continue to dehydrate for 10 to 20 hours longer, or until the tomato slices are completely dry.

Cool completely. Stored in a sealed glass jar or zipper-lock plastic bag at room temperature, dehydrated tomatoes will keep indefinitely.

2 to 3 cups sun-dried tomatoes (not packed in oil)

8 to 10 ripe plum or Roma tomatoes, coarsely chopped

¼ small onion

¼ cup fresh basil leaves, loosely packed

2 tablespoons extra-virgin olive oil

2 sprigs fresh parsley

2 cloves garlic, crushed or chopped

4 fresh oregano leaves, or ½ teaspoon dried oregano

½ teaspoon sea salt

½ teaspoon Italian seasoning

2 pitted soft dates (optional)

▶ **FOR THE MARINARA SAUCE,** soak the sun-dried tomatoes in water to cover for 2 hours, or until softened. Drain well but reserve the liquid (it can be used to thin the sauce later if necessary).

Place the fresh tomatoes in a blender and process until smooth. This should make about 3 cups of tomato purée; if necessary, process additional tomatoes until you have 3 cups. Add some of the soaked sun-dried tomatoes and process until the mixture is thick and dark red. For a richer, thicker sauce, add more of the sun-dried tomatoes and process again until smooth. Add the onion, basil, oil, parsley, garlic, oregano, salt, and Italian herbs to taste and process again. Taste and adjust the seasonings if necessary. If some sweetness is needed, add 1 of the dates and process until smooth. Taste and add the other date if more sweetness is needed.

NOTE: With a high-performance blender, you can add the sun-dried tomatoes without soaking them first. This will create a stronger tomato flavor.

Creamy Tomato Lasagne

See photo facing page 22.

Yield: 8 to 10 servings

There are many ways to make raw lasagne. Our Creamy Tomato Lasagne consists of five separate but simple recipes that are layered to create the final dish. Thinly sliced and marinated zucchini form the "noodles," and three luscious flavor layers, each made with a white sauce base, go in between them; then a marinara sauce tops it all off.

Lasagne tastes best when it is made a day in advance. This not only saves you time, it reduces stress the day of the event. Even better, the five simple recipes can be made two or three days before you assemble the lasagne. By breaking the recipe into easy steps that can be completed over the course of several days, you can have a phenomenal main dish and still be a relaxed host.

The quantities listed in this recipe will make 8 to 10 individual lasagne, each about 3 to 4 inches square and about ¾ inch high. If you would rather not make individual lasagne, you can prepare the recipe in a large lasagne dish and cut it into individual servings.

Moisture control is extremely important with this recipe. If the zucchini is not well marinated and thoroughly dried, the lasagne will create a pool of liquid on the serving plate, which is not desirable. To ensure the best outcome, we recommend that you make the lasagne the day before your event, dehydrate them for two hours (at 105 to 115 degrees F), allow them to return to room temperature, then refrigerate them, and serve them at room temperature the next day. This will create a tasty dish with no excess moisture.

If you don't have a dehydrator, make the lasagne the day before the event, allow the flavors to marry by letting them rest at room temperature for 30 minutes to 2 hours, then refrigerate. Bring the lasagne to room temperature before serving. If you can't make the lasagne the day before your event, prepare them early on the day of your event, then dehydrate them for 2 hours (at 105 to 115 degrees F) and serve. Making individual lasagne isn't difficult, but it is a bit time-consuming. To speed up the process, ask a friend or two to help with the assembly.

WHITE SAUCE

Preparation time: 20 minutes (plus 2 to 3 hours thickening time in the refrigerator)

This sauce is used on its own in the lasagne, and it is also a base for the Green Herb Sauce and the Creamy Tomato Sauce. It can be made two to three days before you assemble the lasagne. White Sauce needs two to three hours to thicken in the refrigerator after it's made. The use of nutritional yeast is optional because it is not raw; however, it adds a great cheesy flavor to the sauce, so we recommend it.

2 cups raw macadamia nuts

2 cups raw cashews

1 cup raw pine nuts

2 cups water, or more as needed

4 lemons, juiced

3 tablespoons nutritional yeast (optional)

1 tablespoon Nama Shoyu, or pinch of sea salt

▶ **FOR THE WHITE SAUCE,** soak the macadamia nuts, cashews, and pine nuts in water to cover for 2 hours. Drain, rinse well, and drain again.

Place the soaked nuts, the 2 cups of water, and the remaining ingredients in a blender and process until smooth. If using salt, season to taste. Refrigerate for 2 to 3 hours until thickened. The sauce should be the consistency of thick sour cream; if it is too thick, thin it with a small amount of additional water.

GREEN HERB SAUCE

Preparation time: 20 minutes (plus advance preparation of the White Sauce)

2 bunches spinach or other mild greens of choice

8 fresh oregano leaves

6 to 8 fresh basil leaves

½ cup White Sauce (see above), or more as needed

▶ **FOR THE GREEN HERB SAUCE,** finely chop the spinach, oregano, and basil (this should yield about 1½ cups). Transfer to a medium-size bowl and stir in just enough White Sauce to bind the ingredients together. Cover tightly and store in the refrigerator until you assemble the lasagne.

CREAMY TOMATO SAUCE

See photo facing page 22.

Preparation time: 15 minutes (plus advance preparation of the White Sauce)

The tomatoes may be prepared two days in advance, but mix them with the White Sauce just before you assemble the lasagne.

8 ripe plum or Roma tomatoes, seeded and finely chopped

1 tablespoon plus 1 teaspoon sea salt

6 to 8 tablespoons White Sauce (page 19)

▶ **FOR THE CREAMY TOMATO SAUCE,** stir the sea salt into the tomatoes and transfer to a colander or fine-mesh strainer. Allow to drain 6 to 12 hours. Then drain very thoroughly on paper towels. For the best results, after the tomatoes have drained on paper towels, wrap them in dry paper towels and place them in an open plastic bag. Refrigerate until just before you assemble the lasagne. Remove from the refrigerator, transfer to a bowl, and stir in the White Sauce, using just enough to bind the ingredients together.

NOTE: For a successful outcome, it is essential that the tomatoes are thoroughly drained and as dry as possible. If you own a dehydrator, blot the tomatoes thoroughly and place them in the dehydrator at 105 to 115 degrees F for about 30 minutes—just long enough to dry them but not dehydrate them.

RED SAUCE

See photo facing page 22.

Preparation time: 20 minutes (plus advance soaking time and additional draining time)

ake this sauce two days before assembling the lasagne. We recommend Medjool dates and kalamata olives for this recipe.

2 cups sun-dried tomatoes (not packed in oil)

8 ripe plum or Roma tomatoes, seeded and coarsely chopped

¼ cup extra-virgin olive oil

4 pitted soft dates

4 pitted olives

1 tablespoon Nama Shoyu

1 teaspoon sea salt

2 cloves garlic (optional; crush or coarsely chop if using a regular home blender)

6 fresh basil leaves

2 fresh oregano leaves

▶ **FOR THE RED SAUCE,** soak the sun-dried tomatoes in water to cover for 2 hours, or until softened. Drain well but reserve the soaking liquid (it can be used to thin the sauce later if necessary).

Transfer the sun-dried tomatoes to a blender and add all of the remaining ingredients. Process until smooth, adding a small amount of the tomato soaking water only if necessary to facilitate processing. Taste and adjust the seasonings if needed.

Transfer the sauce to a fine-mesh strainer or nut milk bag and drain; stir and press the sauce to extract as much extra liquid as possible. Set aside and let drain for 2 to 3 hours.

NOTE: If you are using a nut milk bag to drain the sauce, you can hang it over a bowl and place it in the refrigerator for 2 to 3 hours.

ZUCCHINI NOODLES

See photo, facing page.

Preparation time: 30 minutes (plus marinating time)

Zucchini Noodles need to marinate at for a minimum of eight hours or up to two days.

MARINADE

½ cup extra-virgin olive oil

½ cup freshly squeezed lemon juice or apple cider vinegar

¼ cup Nama Shoyu

2 teaspoons sea salt

2 teaspoons Italian seasoning

4 medium zucchini

▶ **FOR THE MARINADE,** combine the oil, lemon juice, Nama Shoyu, salt, and Italian seasoning in a shallow dish and stir with a fork.

For the noodles, slice off and discard the ends of the zucchini. Slice the zucchini lengthwise very thinly using a mandoline on the thinnest setting or with a sharp knife. Add to the marinade and gently toss until each piece is well coated. Cover and refrigerate for 8 to 48 hours, tossing occasionally. Bring to room temperature before you assemble the lasagne.

How to Assemble Individual Lasagne

For each lasagne, arrange 3 slices of the marinated zucchini side by side in the center of a dinner plate, overlapping them very slightly. Spread a very thin coating of the White Sauce over the zucchini, leaving a 1-inch margin at the top and bottom and a ⅛-inch margin on the sides. Place 3 to 4 tablespoons of the Creamy Tomato Sauce in the center and spread it evenly over the White Sauce. Turn up both ends of each zucchini slice about 1 inch and fold them over the top layer of sauce. Press gently. Use a bit of extra White Sauce, if necessary, to help glue down the ends. Spread 3 to 4 tablespoons of the Green Herb Sauce evenly on top, leaving a ⅛-inch margin on the sides and a ¼-inch margin on the folded ends. Spread 3 to 4 tablespoons of the Red Sauce evenly over the previous layer.

Cover and place directly in the refrigerator, or let rest at room temperature for 30 minutes (to allow the flavors to marry), then cover and refrigerate. Alternatively, dehydrate the lasagne for 2 hours at 105 to 115 degrees F, allow to cool to room temperature, then cover and refrigerate. Dehydrating will prevent the vegetables from weeping and will aid in melding the flavors.

Take the lasagne out of the refrigerator 2 hours before serving to bring it to room temperature. Just before serving, spread the remaining White Sauce over the top. For the most attractive finish, use a frosting tube or

(recipe continued, p. 23)

Creamy Tomato Lasagne, p. 18

Zucchini Pasta, p. 14, with Pesto, p. 15, and Marinara Sauce, p. 16

Meng Khum, p. 33

Thai Tea, p. 32

Thai Coconut Soup, p. 36

Banana-Papaya Pudding, p. 46

Chocolate-Caramel Divine Cheesecake, p. 24

Lemon Gelato. p. 25

piping bag to apply the White Sauce. Alternatively, place the White Sauce in a zipper-lock plastic bag and cut out a small piece of the corner. Squeeze out decorative lines of the White Sauce over the top of the lasagne. For an especially pleasing look, work on the diagonal and create wavy lines. If you like, decorate each serving with 1 or 2 fresh oregano or basil leaves.

Notes

- If you are serving 8 to 10 people, you will need room in your refrigerator to store 8 to 10 plates with lasagne on them.

- If you are just making the lasagne on its own, not as part of a larger meal, these quantities will feed fewer people, so you could plan to serve a large salad and an appetizer or double the ingredients and double the lasagne layers.

How to Assemble a Single Pan of Lasagne

Although any size pan will do, one that works especially well is a 9.5 x 13 x 2-inch pan. We recommend using a glass or decorative ceramic pan.

Arrange half of the marinated zucchini slices, side by side, in a single layer over the bottom of the pan, overlapping them very slightly. Spread a very thin coating of the White Sauce over the zucchini. Place half of the Creamy Tomato Sauce in the center and spread it evenly over the White Sauce. Spread half of the Green Herb Sauce evenly on top. Then spread half of the Red Sauce evenly over the previous layer. Repeat all these layers, starting with zucchini noodles and ending with a final topping of Red Sauce.

Cover and place directly in the refrigerator, or let rest at room temperature for 30 minutes (to allow the flavors to marry), drain off any liquid, then cover and refrigerate.

To serve, bring the lasagne to room temperature, drain off any liquid, and spread the remaining White Sauce over the top just prior to serving. For the most attractive finish, use a frosting tube or piping bag to apply the White Sauce. Alternatively, place the White Sauce in a zipper-lock plastic bag and cut out a small piece of the corner. Squeeze out decorative lines of the White Sauce over the top of the lasagne. For an especially pleasing look, work on the diagonal and create wavy lines. If you like, decorate each serving with 1 or 2 fresh oregano or basil leaves.

NOTE: A full pan of lasagne is too heavy to put in a dehydrator and could damage or break it. For a drier lasagne, dehydrate the marinated zucchini for 20 minutes and the tomatoes for 20 to 30 minutes (both at 105 to 115 degrees F) prior to assembling the lasagne.

Chocolate-Caramel Divine Cheesecake

See photo between pages 22 and 23.   **Preparation time:** 30 minutes (plus advance soaking time)   **Yield:** 8 to 10 servings

This cheesecake is rich and flavorful and is sure to be a hit at any party. It can be made a week or two in advance and stored in the freezer.

CRUST

2 cups raw pecans

½ cup raisins

1 tablespoon currants (optional)

2 tablespoons raw cocoa butter, melted over a bowl of hot water

FILLING

3 cups raw cashews

1 vanilla bean

½ cup raw cocoa butter, melted over a bowl of hot water

¾ cup freshly squeezed lemon juice

½ to ¾ cup dark agave syrup

¼ cup coconut oil

½ teaspoon sea salt

TOPPING

½ cup raw cocoa powder

¼ cup raw cocoa butter, melted over a bowl of hot water

2 teaspoons agave syrup

▶ **FOR THE CRUST,** place all of the ingredients in a food processor fitted with the S blade and process until the mixture is crumbly and holds together when pinched between your fingers. Don't overprocess it; a little texture is pleasing to the palate and adds visual appeal. Press the mixture evenly into the bottom of a springform pan.

▶ **FOR THE FILLING,** soak the cashews for 3 to 5 hours in water to cover. Drain, rinse well, and drain again. Grind the vanilla bean in a coffee grinder or spice grinder. If you don't have a grinder, simply slit open the vanilla bean lengthwise and scrape out the pulp and seeds with a spoon, and discard the outer pod. Combine all of the ingredients in a blender and process until completely smooth. Pour evenly over the crust.

▶ **FOR THE TOPPING,** combine all of the ingredients in a small bowl and stir until well combined. Drizzle over the cake. If you are making the cake several days or a week or so in advance, put the cake in the freezer and move it to the refrigerator 3 to 4 hours before serving. If you are making the cake the day before your event, just refrigerate it until serving time. Slice it while it is still firm.

Lemon Gelato

See photo facing page 23. **Preparation time:** 45 minutes (plus freezing time)   **Yield:** 8 to 10 servings

This dessert is light and refreshing with a lemony tang. It makes a great ending to any meal. Prepare this recipe the night before your event. Don't make it too far in advance, though, because it will become hard and require processing to soften. Lemon Gelato looks refreshing served in a small bowl with lemon zest shavings on top.

2 cups water

2 cups young coconut flesh

1½ cups freshly squeezed lemon juice

1½ cups light agave syrup

▶ Combine all of the ingredients in a blender and process until smooth. Chill it in the freezer for about 1 hour, then transfer to an ice cream maker and process according to the manufacturer's instructions. Alternatively, simply freeze the gelato for 12 to 24 hours. The mixture should not be rock solid. If it does freeze too hard, scoop it into a food processor fitted with the S blade, process until it is softened, then put it back in the freezer until serving time.

Notes

- Use only light agave syrup for this recipe. Amber or dark agave syrup will discolor the gelato and overwhelm the lemon flavor.
- A fun way to serve Lemon Gelato is in lemon cups. To make them, cut lemons in half widthwise, juice them, and freeze the lemon shells in a zipper-lock bag. When you are ready to serve the dessert, fill the cups with Lemon Gelato, put them on a plate, and garnish with a twist of lemon rind on top.

THAI

Menu

Thai Tea

Meng Khum (Savory-Sweet
Thai Parcels)

Thai Coconut Soup

Thai Cucumber Salad

Pad Thai Noodles

Mango-Banana Custard

Equipment Needed

blender

citrus juicer or reamer

nut milk bag or fine-mesh strainer

vegetable peeler

Thai Menu

Authentic Thai food combines a perfectly balanced mix of fives tastes: salty, sweet, spicy, bitter, and sour. We capture these traditional flavors in our Thai recipes with raw vegan ingredients like salty dulse, sweet agave syrup, spicy chiles, bitter greens, and sour lime.

We recommend serving the courses for this Thai meal in the following order. First serve Thai Tea and Meng Khum. Next, serve individual bowls of Thai Coconut Soup and place the Cucumber Salad and Pad Thai Noodles in serving bowls on the table for guests to help themselves (for a lighter meal, serve only two of these rather than all three). Then, after a conversation break, serve the Mango-Banana Custard for dessert, perhaps with some more Thai Tea.

The emphasis in Thai cuisine is on crisp, fresh ingredients. For this reason, most of the food must be prepared no sooner than one day before it will be served. When broken down into steps, the preparation is quite simple. If you are organized, it should only take about three hours to prepare the entire meal (maybe four if you count cleaning up). With your first attempt at this menu, definitely allow some extra time for yourself. Practice making the basil cups and cracking open mature coconuts ahead of time.

Two days before your event:

- do all of your grocery shopping

One day before your event:

- make Thai Tea (page 32)
- make the filling for Meng Khum (page 33)
- make Thai Cucumber Salad (page 34)
- make Pad Thai Sauce (page 35)
- set out serving dishes, flatware, and tablecloths

Sweet Raisin Water

In many raw food recipes, dates or dried fruits are used for sweetening. In delicate dishes, however, the flavor of blended dried fruit can be overwhelming. An easy alternative is to use Sweet Raisin Water instead. Simply combine 2 cups of raisins with 2 cups of water in a jar or bowl (add a little more water if your raisins are especially dry) and allow to rest for 24 to 48 hours in the refrigerator. Drain the raisins and save the water, which will be very sweet. Use the raisins for another recipe. Store leftover Sweet Raisin Water in the refrigerator.

The day of your event:

- make Noodle Salad (page 35)

  Note: If it will be longer than 4 hours before serving time, the carrots for the Noodle Salad can be julienned and put in a bowl of cold water in the refrigerator to stay fresh and crisp. Drain the carrots well before adding them to the Noodle Salad.

- prepare the garnish for the Pad Thai Noodles (page 35)
- make Thai Coconut Soup Broth (page 36) and refrigerate (the broth will solidify when cold; it will become fluid again when it is warmed)

- prepare the vegetables for the Thai Coconut Soup (page 36)

  Note: Store the prepared vegetables in a sealed container in the refrigerator and bring them to room temperature about one hour before using. If serving time is less than four hours away, leave the prepared vegetables in a covered container on the countertop, as they are best served at room temperature. If you prefer to dice the avocado in advance (rather than just before serving), sprinkle it with a bit of lime juice to keep it from discoloring.

- make Mango-Banana Custard (page 37)

Just before serving the meal:

- prepare the basil cups for the Meng Khum (page 33), fill them, and arrange them on a serving platter (if you are adept at making and filling the basil cups, try doing it in front of your company; it will be one less detail to take care of before they arrive, and it will be entertaining)

Thai Tea

See photo between pages 54 and 55.   **Preparation time:** 10 minutes   **Yield:** 8 to 10 servings

This light, refreshing drink is reminiscent of iced tea. It's the perfect complement to a spicy meal, or serve it as a cooling beverage on a hot day. You can make Thai Tea one day in advance and keep it chilled in the refrigerator.

8 cups water

32 fresh basil leaves

6 tablespoons freshly squeezed lemon juice

6 tablespoons agave syrup or other sweetener of choice

2 tablespoons minced galangal or grated fresh ginger

Slices of lemon or lime

▶ Combine the water, basil, lemon juice, agave syrup, and galangal in a blender and process until well combined. Strain through a nut milk bag or fine-mesh strainer. Pour into tall glasses filled with ice and garnish with a slice of lemon.

How to Choose and Grate a Mature Coconut

Mature coconuts are the brown ones found in most supermarkets. Fresh mature coconut adds better texture and flavor to recipes than packaged dried coconut. A good coconut will have a lot of water inside; shake several to find the best one. Also check that all of the "eyes" at the top of the coconut are firm.

To open the coconut, use a thin knife or Phillips head screwdriver to pierce the softest of the three black "eyes" at the top of the coconut. Invert the coconut over a large glass or bowl to drain the water. Taste the water to make sure it isn't sour or moldy; if it is, discard the coconut and start again with a fresh one. Once the water has been drained, place the coconut in two or three heavy-duty zipper-lock plastic bags and pound it on a driveway or sidewalk until it breaks into pieces. Sheryl's friend Miriam throws coconuts off the second-story deck of her house! Do whatever works. Insert a thin knife between the shell and the meat to pry it off. You can then either grate the meat finely with a cheese grater (save end pieces for another recipe) or in a food processor fitted with the S blade. Special coconut graters can be purchased at Indian grocery stores; they are a great tool to have in a raw food kitchen.

Meng Khum
(SAVORY-SWEET THAI PARCELS)

See photo facing page 54.   **Preparation time:** 35 minutes   **Yield:** 8 to 10 servings

2 cups finely shredded
fresh mature coconut

½ lime, juiced

2 tablespoons dulse flakes

2 cloves garlic, minced

6 tablespoons chopped
green onions

½ red bell pepper,
chopped

32 large basil leaves or
baby spinach leaves with
stem

2 tablespoons agave syrup

These sweet-and-savory nibbles are a favorite Thai appetizer. They can be filled with a variety of mixtures, but the underlying flavor theme is always sweet and savory. The traditional Thai recipe calls for banana leaves, but you can substitute sweet basil or baby spinach leaves. The filling and garnish may be prepared a day in advance, but the leaves must be filled and folded just before serving to prevent the parcels from discoloring.

▶ Combine the coconut, lime juice, dulse, garlic, and 2 tablespoons of the green onions in a bowl. In a separate bowl, combine the bell pepper and the remaining 4 tablespoons of green onions.

Fold the basil leaves into little cups (see below for photos and step-by-step directions). Spoon about 1 teaspoon of the coconut mixture into each folded leaf. Garnish with some of the bell pepper mixture and drizzle with agave syrup.

NOTE: Unsweetened shredded dried coconut may be substituted for fresh mature coconut if necessary, but the results won't be as good.

How to Fold Basil Leaves or Baby Spinach Leaves into Cups

There is an art to folding leaves into cups; it's a good idea to practice before the day of your event. Once you have the knack of it, they are quite easy to make. Choose medium-large to large leaves. Be sure each leaf has a long, intact stem, as it will be used to hold the cup together. Gently fold the stem sideways toward the other side of the leaf. Twist the stem around and poke the end of it through the leaf to hold the cup together. Press lightly from the inside to open up the cup. If you fill the cups soon after you make them they will hold their shape better. Here is a step-by-step process for how to fold the cups.

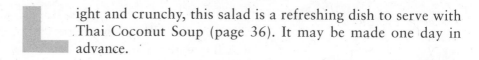

Thai Cucumber Salad

Preparation time: 25 minutes

Yield: 8 to 10 servings

Light and crunchy, this salad is a refreshing dish to serve with Thai Coconut Soup (page 36). It may be made one day in advance.

6 Kirby cucumbers or other small cucumbers, thinly sliced

1 red bell pepper, sliced

2 limes, juiced

4 green onions, chopped

2 tablespoons coarsely chopped fresh cilantro leaves

2 tablespoons light agave syrup

▶ Combine all of the ingredients in a bowl. Cover and chill in the refrigerator until serving time.

Pad Thai Noodles

Preparation time: 40 minutes

Yield: 8 to 10 servings

This Pad Thai is made up of three simple recipes: noodle salad, sauce, and garnish. The secret to its success is the thick zucchini noodles. Made with a vegetable peeler, they are similar to thick, flat rice noodles. They stand out beautifully and hold the sauce well.

NOODLE SALAD

4 medium to large zucchini

2 large carrots

½ cup coarsely chopped fresh cilantro leaves

½ cup fresh bean sprouts

PAD THAI SAUCE

2 cups raw almond butter

2 oranges, juiced

1 lemon, juiced

1 lime, juiced

4 cloves garlic, minced

8 pitted soft dates

2 tablespoons grated fresh ginger

2 teaspoons sea salt

1 small hot red chile, minced, or 2 teaspoons crushed dried chiles (optional)

GARNISH

4 green onions, chopped

4 tablespoons chopped Thai basil or other type of fresh basil

10 to 12 wedges fresh lime

8 raw almonds, chopped

▶ **FOR THE SALAD,** peel the zucchini, then shave the flesh into thick strips with a vegetable peeler. Cut the carrots into thin matchsticks (julienne) with either a mandoline or a sharp knife. Combine the zucchini, carrots, cilantro, and bean sprouts in a bowl and toss together gently.

▶ **FOR THE SAUCE,** combine all of the ingredients in a blender and process until smooth. If necessary, add a small amount of water to facilitate blending. The sauce should be thick. Add the sauce to the noodle salad and mix well.

NOTE: If you are using a high-performance blender, you may replace the almond butter with 2½ cups of raw almonds. Add them to the blender along with all of the other sauce ingredients, and process until smooth.

▶ **FOR THE GARNISH,** sprinkle the green onions, basil, lime wedges, and almonds over the salad just before serving.

Thai Coconut Soup

See photo between pages 54 and 55. **Preparation time:** 45 minutes   **Yield:** 8 to 10 servings

T his is a rich, hearty, and flavorful soup that is made in two steps. First the broth is blended, then the vegetables are arranged in serving bowls and the broth is poured over them. Make this soup just before serving it.

SOUP BROTH

2 mature coconuts, including the water

2 stalks lemongrass

½ red bell pepper

¼ cup freshly squeezed lime juice, or 2 kaffir lime leaves

2 to 3 small hot red chiles, or 1 to 3 teaspoons crushed dried chiles

1 (2-inch) cube fresh galangal or ginger, peeled

2 teaspoons sea salt

2 cloves garlic, crushed or chopped

VEGETABLES

4 medium-size carrots, julienned or spiralized

2 ripe avocados

1 red onion, thinly sliced

1 cup snow peas, thinly sliced on the diagonal

½ cup fresh cilantro leaves

FOR THE SOUP BROTH, pour the coconut water into a measuring cup and add additional water as needed to make 6 cups in all. Transfer to a blender and add the coconut meat. Coarsely chop the tender portions of the lemongrass and add to the blender. Process until smooth. Add the remaining ingredients and process again until smooth. Strain through a nut milk bag or fine-mesh strainer. Discard the pulp. If you want warm soup, blend a final time at high speed until the mixture is warmed; then serve immediately. (If you do not have a high-performance blender, you can warm the soup over very low heat in a saucepan on the stove; watch carefully to make sure it is heated just until it is warm to the touch.)

Notes

- If the coconut water tastes sour or unpleasant, discard the coconut and water and use another coconut. Because it is impossible to tell the age or quality of a coconut until it has been opened, we recommend purchasing several extras in case you run into this situation.
- Running the blender for an extra few minutes creates enough friction to warm the soup. Be careful not to make the soup too warm; under 115 degree F is optimal to retain all of the nutrients.

FOR THE VEGETABLES, distribute the carrots, avocado, onion, snow peas, and cilantro among 8 to 10 soup bowls. Pour the warm soup over the vegetables. Serve immediately.

NOTE: Excessive amounts of mature coconut can have a laxative effect on some people. Although this soup is so delicious you may be tempted to eat the entire recipe by yourself, resist!

Mango-Banana Custard

Preparation time: 20 minutes

This custard is silky smooth and delicious. Traditional Thai custard is made with eggs, but for this recipe we have replaced the eggs with macadamia nuts for similar richness and mouthfeel. If you prefer, cashews also work well. Make this custard within a few hours of serving to avoid oxidation and darkening of the fruits.

PUDDING

6 large ripe bananas

4 ripe mangos

⅔ cup raw macadamia nuts or cashews

1 vanilla bean

GARNISH (Optional)

Grated vanilla bean, vanilla seeds, or chopped mango

▶ **FOR THE PUDDING,** place 5 of the bananas in a blender. Add the mango, nuts, and whole vanilla bean. If you don't have a high-performance blender, grind the vanilla bean in a spice grinder or coffee grinder before adding it to the blender. If you don't have either of these, just cut open the vanilla bean and scrape out the seeds and pulp with the tip of a spoon and discard the outer pod. Process until completely smooth.

Slice the remaining banana and distribute it equally among 4 serving bowls. Pour the pudding over the sliced banana, add the optional garnish of your choice, and serve immediately.

When making any recipe that calls for bananas, be sure to shop several days before your event so the bananas are ripe and ready when you need them.

BRUNCH

Brunch Menu

Menu

Vanilla Nut Nog

Apple-Cranberry Juice or Citrus-Cranberry Juice

Banana-Papaya Pudding or Banana-Avocado Pudding, with Cashew Cream

Oatmeal with Dates and Almonds or Sweet Buckwheat Cereal

Fruit Kabobs or Platter of Seasonal Fruits with Berry Dressing

Apple-Cranberry Tart

Equipment Needed

blender

citrus juicer or reamer

food processor

juicer

nut milk bag or fine-mesh strainer

wooden skewers or lemongrass stalks

For this brunch menu we provide several options for most of the recipes. This is because we want to ensure that, regardless of your locale or the time of year, you will have access to seasonal fruit. We also provide alternative preparation suggestions for recipes that call for a dehydrator in case you do not own one.

Two weeks before your event:

- make Sweet Buckwheat Cereal (page 48)

Three days before your event:

- do all of your grocery shopping
- begin soaking the raw oat groats for Oatmeal with Dates and Almonds (page 47)

Two days before your event:

- begin soaking the ingredients for Vanilla Nut Nog (page 43)
- make Cashew Cream (page 45)

One day before your event:

- make Apple-Cranberry Tart (page 51)
- make Vanilla Nut Nog (page 43)
- make Oatmeal with Dates and Almonds (page 47); omit the bananas
- make Berry Dressing (page 49)
- set out serving dishes, flatware, and table-cloths

The day of your event:
four hours in advance

- prepare Fruit Kabobs (page 50) or Platter of Seasonal Fruits (page 49)

three hours in advance

- make Banana-Papaya Pudding (page 46) or Banana-Avocado Pudding (page 45)
- stir the bananas into the Oatmeal with Dates and Almonds

one hour in advance

- make Apple-Cranberry Juice (page 44) or Citrus-Cranberry Juice (page 44)

Serving Suggestions

If you are serving more than 8 to 10 people for brunch, you can increase the amounts in the recipes or use more than one of the suggested options for a larger variety of food. As your guests arrive, serve them fresh juice or Vanilla Nut Nog, or lead them to where it is waiting for them in glasses or in a pitcher on ice. While champagne flutes layered with orange or green pudding and Cashew Cream look inviting, if you don't have the time to make them or you don't have enough wine glasses or glass flutes (the lightweight plastic ones might tip over, so we don't recommend using them), or the crowd you have invited is just too large to make it practical, have no fear! A large serving bowl of pudding with a dollop of Cashew Cream on top, surrounded by individual dessert bowls and spoons, also makes for a lovely table setting. Try using china teacups instead of dessert bowls—they are both fun and pretty to look at.

Preparation times are based on 8 to 10 servings per recipe and the use of a high-performance blender. If you are using a regular home blender, your preparation times will be longer.

Vanilla Nut Nog

Preparation time: 1 hour (plus advance soaking time)   **Yield:** 8 to 10 servings (about 7½ cups)

Similar to eggnog, this beverage is rich and creamy, and the flavor of the Brazil nuts complements the spices beautifully. Whether you have a high-performance blender or a regular home blender, you will have the best success if you prepare the nog in batches. For convenience and the best taste, make the nog one day in advance of your event.

5 cups raw Brazil nuts

30 to 40 pitted Medjool dates

5 vanilla beans, or 2 tablespoons vanilla extract

9 to 11 cups water

¾ teaspoon ground cinnamon

Grated nutmeg

▶ Soak the Brazil nuts in water to cover for 8 to 12 hours. In a separate bowl, soak the dates and vanilla beans (or vanilla extract) together in water to cover for 8 to 12 hours.

Drain the Brazil nuts, rinse well, and drain again. Remove the dates and vanilla beans from the soaking water and add enough additional water to measure 10 cups. Pour into a blender, add the Brazil nuts, and process until smooth. Add the dates, vanilla beans, and cinnamon to the blender. Process again until smooth, stopping occasionally to scrape down the sides of the container. The mixture will be quite thick; if you prefer a thinner nog, add up to 1 more cup of water and process again. Taste and add more dates, vanilla beans or vanilla extract, and/or cinnamon as desired and process until smooth.

Place the nut milk bag in a large bowl, pour the blended mixture into it in batches, and gently squeeze out the liquid. Pour the strained nog into clear cups, grate a bit of fresh nutmeg on the top, and enjoy.

NOTE: If you are using a regular home blender, you can make enough Vanilla Nut Nog for your crowd by blending small batches that make 1 to 2 servings until you have the quantity that you need. To make 1 to 2 servings at a time use ½ cup Brazil nuts (soaked 8 to 12 hours), 4 pitted Medjool dates, ½ vanilla bean or 1 teaspoon vanilla extract (soak the dates and vanilla bean or vanilla extract together for 8 to 12 hours), a pinch of cinnamon, and enough water added to the date soaking water to measure 1 cup.

Apple-Cranberry Juice

Preparation time: 40 minutes

Yield: 8 to 10 servings

24 to 40 medium-size apples

24 to 40 fresh cranberries

▶ Process the fruit through a juicer 1 hour before your guests arrive. Chill thoroughly before serving.

NOTE: For a larger or smaller crowd, calculate the amounts you need per person. For each serving use 3 to 4 small to medium apples and 3 to 4 fresh cranberries.

Citrus-Cranberry Juice

Preparation time: 40 minutes

Yield: 8 to 10 servings

ake this juice no sooner than one hour before guests arrive, as citrus juice can become bitter if it sits for too long. Use a combination of oranges, tangerines, and grapefruit.

24 to 40 citrus fruits (any kind except lemons or limes)

1 lemon

⅔ cup fresh or frozen cranberries

▶ Juice all the citrus fruits with an electric or manual citrus juicer. Transfer 1 to 2 cups of the juice to a blender, add the cranberries, and process until smooth. Strain the cranberry mixture through a nut milk bag or fine-mesh strainer. Combine the citrus and cranberry juices. Alternatively, peel the citrus fruits, remove all of the white pith, and process the citrus fruit and cranberries through a heavy-duty juicer. Chill thoroughly before serving.

VARIATION: If you can't find cranberries, substitute fresh or frozen raspberries.

NOTE: For a larger or smaller crowd, calculate the amounts you need per person. Use 2 to 3 citrus fruits and about 6 cranberries per serving, with 1 lemon per 10 servings.

Banana-Avocado Pudding

Preparation time: 25 minutes

Yield: 8 to 10 servings

This luscious pudding has a beautiful green color. Plan for extra preparation time if you are serving the pudding in wine glasses or champagne flutes.

8 to 10 ripe bananas

4 to 5 ripe avocados

1¾ cups Cashew Cream (see below), as needed

▶ Combine the bananas and avocados in a blender and process until smooth. (You may need to process the mixture in batches depending on the size and power of your blender.) Serve in a large, attractive serving bowl and top with Cashew Cream. Alternatively, layer the pudding in wine glasses or champagne flutes alternating it with layers of Cashew Cream.

CASHEW CREAM

Preparation time: 15 minutes (plus advance soaking time)

Yield: 8 to 10 servings (about 1¾ cups)

Better than whipped cream, Cashew Cream is smooth, sweet, and rich. It's sure to become a favorite. Although the preparation time is minimal, the cashews and dates must be soaked in advance.

1 cup raw cashews

4 pitted Medjool dates

Small piece vanilla bean, or 1 teaspoon vanilla extract

▶ Soak the cashews for 8 to 12 hours in water to cover. In a separate bowl, soak the dates and vanilla bean (or vanilla extract) together in water to cover plus 2 inches for 8 to 12 hours.

Drain the cashews, rinse well, and drain again. Place the cashews in a blender. Remove the dates and vanilla bean from the soaking water. Add just enough of the date soaking water to barely cover the cashews in the blender and process until smooth and thick; the consistency should be similar to whipped cream. Add the dates and vanilla bean, if using, and process again until smooth.

VARIATION: Replace the cashews with 1 cup of raw macadamia nuts. Soak and process as directed.

Banana-Papaya Pudding

See photo facing page 55. **Preparation time:** 25 minutes

Yield: 8 to 10 servings

This pudding is made simply from ripe fresh fruit. For a richer, creamier pudding, add the optional tahini. Plan for extra preparation time if you are serving the pudding in wine glasses or champagne flutes.

8 to 10 ripe bananas

8 to 10 cups chopped ripe papaya

3 to 7 tablespoons raw tahini (optional)

1¾ cups Cashew Cream (page 45), as needed

▶ Combine the bananas, papaya, and optional tahini in a blender and process until smooth. (You may need to process the mixture in batches depending on the size and power of your blender.) Serve in a large, attractive serving bowl and top with Cashew Cream. Alternatively, layer the pudding in wine glasses or champagne flutes alternating it with layers of Cashew Cream.

Presentation of the Pudding

To layer the pudding in a wine glass or champagne flute, first put in a thick layer of pudding and top it with a thin layer of Cashew Cream. Continue layering in this fashion, alternating layers of the pudding and Cashew Cream, until you have almost reached the top of the glass. Finish with a dollop of Cashew Cream. If you prefer, alternate layers of pudding and chopped nuts, finishing with a dollop of Cashew Cream and a sprinkling of chopped nuts. For even more visual and taste excitement, try layering in a little Berry Dressing (page 49); it will add a beautiful contrasting color to this special dessert.

If you are serving the pudding in a large bowl, you can omit the Cashew Cream or cut the amount in half. Simply place a large dollop of the Cashew Cream in the center of the bowl of pudding.

Oatmeal with Dates and Almonds

Preparation time: 10 minutes (plus advance soaking time)   **Yield:** 8 to 10 servings

Raw oat groats are a little difficult to find, so you may have to order them by mail. Most oat groats are steam treated to "stabilize" them to keep them from spoiling. The best places to look for raw oat groats are online retailers that sell raw nuts, seeds, and grains for sprouting. Although this recipe takes very little time to prepare, the oat groats must be soaked for 48 hours or longer in advance.

2½ cups raw oat groats, soaked for 48 hours or longer in the refrigerator (change the water every 8 hours)

1¼ cups raw almonds, soaked for 8 to 12 hours

10 pitted dates or figs, soaked for 8 to 12 hours in water to cover plus 2 inches

¾ teaspoon ground cinnamon

2½ ripe bananas, or 2 to 3 coarsely chopped apples

Drain the oat groats, rinse well, and drain again. Drain the almonds, rinse well, and drain again. Place the oat groats and almonds in a blender. Add the dates, the date soaking water, and the cinnamon to the blender and process until smooth, adding small amounts of additional water to facilitate blending if necessary. Add the bananas and pulse just until they are coarsely chopped.

Notes

- If you are using a regular home blender, process this recipe in small batches that make 2 servings each until you have the quantity you need. For each batch use approximately ½ cup soaked oats groats, ¼ cup soaked almonds, 2 soaked dates, ½ banana, and a dash of cinnamon.

- If you cannot find raw oat groats, you can make this recipe with other whole grains such as barley, kamut berries, or spelt berries.

- The cereal can be made up to 24 hours before your event, but add the banana or apple just before serving. The banana or apple may be coarsely chopped by hand and stirred in.

Sweet Buckwheat Cereal

Preparation time: 30 minutes (plus advance soaking time)

Yield: 8 to 10 servings (about 8 cups)

This cereal is great to make ahead and have ready for a quick breakfast, as it keeps for months. It's also a very flexible recipe; you can add any fruits or nuts that capture your fancy. If the cereal tastes good before it has been dehydrated, you know it will be delicious afterward, once the flavors have been concentrated. Serve it with nut milk and fresh fruit of your choice.

3 cups hulled raw buckwheat groats, soaked for 4 hours (rinse and replace the soaking water several times)

1 cup raw pecans, soaked for 2 hours

1 cup raw sunflower seeds, soaked for 2 hours

2 apples, chopped

2 ripe bananas

1 cup raisins

½ cup agave syrup

2 tablespoons freshly squeezed lemon juice

2 tablespoons orange zest

1 vanilla bean, ground in a spice grinder or coffee grinder, or 1 teaspoon vanilla extract

1 teaspoon ground cinnamon

1 teaspoon sea salt

Drain the buckwheat groats, pecans, and sunflower seeds, rinse well, and drain again. Transfer the buckwheat groats, pecans, and sunflower seeds to a food processor fitted with the S blade. Add all of the remaining ingredients and process until coarsely chopped. Remove half of the mixture and place it in a large bowl. Process the remaining mixture until it is very smooth and add it to the bowl. Mix well.

Spread the mixture thinly on solid (ParaFlexx) dehydrator sheets. Dehydrate at 105 to 115 degrees F for 3 to 4 hours. Flip the mixture onto mesh dehydrator sheets and dehydrate for 12 to 16 hours longer, or until crisp. Let cool, then break into smaller pieces. Store in an airtight container at room temperature.

Notes

- Stored in an airtight container in the pantry, Sweet Buckwheat Cereal will keep for several months (though it's so tasty it will likely last just a few days).

- Buckwheat groats will become mucilaginous when they are soaked. This quality is what makes buckwheat popular for use in dehydrated recipes, as it helps hold the ingredients together. Rinse the buckwheat frequently if it will be soaked for longer than a few hours.

Platter of Seasonal Fruits with Berry Dressing

Preparation time: 30 to 40 minutes

Yield: 8 to 10 servings

What type of fruit you serve depends on the season and where you live. Party guests always appreciate sweet, juicy, tropical fruits like pineapple, papaya, or mango, but apples, bananas, and grapes are also delicious choices. Select the best of what's available for your fruit platter, and place the pretty pink Berry Dressing in a small, clear glass pitcher next to the fruit platter.

8 to 10 seasonal fruits of choice

▶ Cut the fruits into attractive shapes or bite-size pieces and arrange them on a platter. Cover and store in the refrigerator for up to 4 hours before serving.

BERRY DRESSING

See photo facing page 86.

Preparation time: 20 minutes

Yield: 8 to 10 servings

1 tablespoon lemon zest

4 tablespoons freshly squeezed lemon juice

16 medium-size strawberries

40 raspberries

4 tablespoons agave syrup or other sweetener of choice

4 tablespoons flaxseed oil, hempseed oil, or extra-virgin olive oil

4 fresh basil leaves, chopped

Pinch of sea salt

Pinch of freshly ground black pepper (optional)

▶ Remove the lemon zest before juicing the lemons. Transfer the lemon zest, lemon juice, and all of the remaining ingredients to a blender and process until smooth. To remove any seeds from the dressing, strain it through a nut milk bag or fine-mesh strainer.

NOTE: If you are using a regular home blender, if necessary you can process the dressing in 4 small batches using 1 teaspoon lemon zest, 1 tablespoon lemon juice, 4 strawberries, 8 to 10 raspberries, 1 tablespoon agave syrup, 1 tablespoon flaxseed oil, 1 fresh basil leaf, and sea salt and optional black pepper to taste per batch.

Fruit Kabobs

See photo facing page 86.   **Preparation time:** 40 minutes   **Yield:** 8 to 10 servings

This dish offers a hot-and-sweet surprise. If this is your only fruit offering, use one whole fruit per person; if you are serving other fruit dishes, use about half a fruit per person. Select fruits that can be easily cut into pieces. For an epicurean touch, thread the fruit on lemongrass stalks instead of wooden skewers.

4 to 10 whole fruits, cut into bite-size pieces

Freshly squeezed lemon juice

Maple sugar or date sugar

Cayenne

▶ Sprinkle the cut fruit lightly with lemon juice and toss it gently (this will help it to stay fresh longer). Thread the fruit pieces onto wooden skewers or lemongrass stalks, using 3 to 4 different types of fruit per skewer and alternating colors and textures. Arrange the threaded skewers on an attractive serving platter and sprinkle them lightly with maple sugar and cayenne.

NOTE: If using lemongrass stalks, cut the ends on a sharp-angled point to spear the fruit.

Apple-Cranberry Tart

See photo between pages 86 and 87.   **Preparation Time:** 50 minutes (plus advance soaking time) **Yield:** 8 to 10 servings

This recipe has a thick crust that tastes like a shortbread cookie; it is filled first with a layer of Cashew Cream, then topped with a sweetened cranberry-apple mixture. This tart can be served the same day it is made, but it tastes even better when it is prepared the day before your event and refrigerated.

CRUST

3 cups macadamia nuts

4 tablespoons light agave syrup

FILLING

½ cup Cashew Cream (page 45)

TOPPING

4 apples, peeled and coarsely chopped

½ cup fresh or thawed frozen cranberries

¼ cup light agave syrup

2 tablespoons Cashew Cream (page 45)

2 tablespoons psyllium powder

▶ **FOR THE CRUST,** place the macadamia nuts and agave syrup in a food processor fitted with the S blade and process until they are coarsely ground and the mixture holds together. Firmly press into the bottom of a round springform pan to form a thick crust.

▶ **FOR THE FILLING,** spread the ½ cup of Cashew Cream over the crust.

▶ **FOR THE TOPPING,** combine the apples, cranberries, agave syrup, and the 2 tablespoons of Cashew Cream in a blender or food processor fitted with the S blade and process until smooth, stopping frequently to scrape down the sides of the container. Taste for sweetness and tartness, and add more cranberries or agave syrup to suit your taste. With the machine running, gradually add the psyllium powder through the opening in the lid until it is well incorporated. Immediately spread the topping over the filling. Cover and refrigerate.

NOTE: Psyllium powder makes a firmer filling so the tart can be easily sliced. If you don't have psyllium powder on hand, make individual tarts in small ramekins.

COCKTAILS

Menu

Drinks: Strawberry Daiquiris, Ambrosia, Piña Coladas

Fruit Platter with Sweet Dips:

Goji-Orange Sauce

Chocolate-Orange Sauce

Cashew Cream

Vegetable Platter with Savory Dips:

Tomato and Olive Tapenade

Pistachio Pesto

Pâté du Soleil

Japanese Shoyu Dressing

Zucchini Roll-Ups

Zucchini Canapés

Equipment Needed

blender

citrus juicer or reamer

dehydrator (optional)

food processor

juicer (optional)

mandoline (optional)

nut milk bag or fine-mesh strainer

Cocktail Hour Menu

This menu is designed for festive events where drinks and hors d'oeuvres are served. Select the recipes that interest you the most, or go all out and make everything!

4

Four days before your event

- make Pâté du Soleil (page 63)
- make Japanese Shoyu Dressing (page 64)
- make Zucchini Roll-Ups (page 65)

Two days before your event

- do all of your grocery shopping
- begin soaking the ingredients for Cashew Cream (page 45)

One day before your event

- make Tomato and Olive Tapenade (page 62)
- make Cashew Cream (page 45)
- make Goji-Orange Sauce (page 60)
- make Chocolate-Orange Sauce (page 60)
- make Pistachio Pesto (page 62)
- set out serving dishes, flatware, and tablecloths

Serving Suggestions

The Piña Coladas and Ambrosia can be prepared a few hours before your event, although you will need to wait to blend the ice into the Piña Coladas until just before serving. Strawberry Daiquiris are best made fresh. If possible, ask a friend to "tend bar" for you. Placing a slice or two of fruit on the rim of the drink will add even more festive cheer.

The Fruit Platter with Dips is terrific served first with the drinks; serve the Vegetable Platter a little later. Try to allow at least 30 minutes between serving the fruit and the vegetables to aid digestion.

The day of your event

- arrange Fruit Platter (page 59)
- arrange Vegetable Platter (page 61)
- make Zucchini Canapés (page 65)
- make Ambrosia (page 57)

Just before or during your event

- make Strawberry Daiquiris (page 57)
- make Piña Coladas (page 58)

Strawberry Daiquiris

Preparation time: 10 minutes

Yield: 8 to 10 servings

This drink is a taste of summer—just like the freshest tropical drinks served at a resort. Imagine sipping it while sitting on a white sand beach beneath a clear blue sky.

5 cups frozen strawberries

5 cups water

½ cup plus 1 tablespoon light agave syrup

8 to 10 lime slices

▶ Combine the strawberries, water, and agave syrup in a blender and process until smooth. Serve immediately, with a slice of lime on the rim of each glass.

NOTE: If you are using a regular home blender, you will need to process the drink in small batches of 2 servings each until you have the amount you need. For each batch use 1 cup frozen strawberries, 1 cup water, and 2 tablespoons light agave syrup.

Ambrosia

Preparation time: 30 minutes

Yield: 8 to 10 servings

This is a sweet and delicious drink enjoyed by all. Serve it the same day it is made.

1 pineapple

2 pounds grapes

2 oranges, peeled

1 lime, peeled

▶ Juice all of the ingredients in a heavy-duty juicer. Alternatively, peel the pineapple, blend all of the fruit in a high-performance blender, and strain it through a nut milk bag or fine-mesh strainer. Chill thoroughly before serving.

Piña Coladas

A piña colada is a tropical drink made from fresh coconut and pineapple. Although most recipes for this drink contain rum, the traditional version does not, so our interpretation is actually more authentic. Serve it in fancy glasses for a special touch.

2 young coconuts, flesh and water

4 cups fresh pineapple chunks

2 limes, juiced

Pinch of sea salt

1 cup ice

2 to 4 tablespoons agave syrup (optional)

▶ Combine the coconut flesh and water, pineapple, lime juice, and sea salt in a blender and process until smooth. Add the ice and process again. Taste and blend in the optional agave syrup if more sweetness is needed. Serve immediately.

VARIATION: Blend in 1 banana along with the coconut and pineapple for a special flavor twist.

Notes

- If you are using a regular home blender, process the mixture in 2 batches.
- Although mature coconut is more commonly used for this drink, we use young coconut because it makes a lighter beverage that is lower in fat. If you prefer to use mature coconut, put the flesh in a blender and add enough coconut water to just cover it. Process until completely smooth. If necessary, add more coconut water or plain water to facilitate blending. Strain through a nut milk bag or fine-mesh strainer; the resulting liquid is called coconut milk. Use all of the coconut milk to replace the young coconut flesh and water in the recipe.

Fruit Platter with Sweet Dips

Yield: 8 to 10 servings

A platter of fresh fruit served with dipping sauces is sure to please. Plan on one or two pieces of fruit per person, depending on what other dishes you are serving. Serve the platter with one or two dips of your choice: Goji-Orange Sauce, Chocolate-Orange Sauce, or Cashew Cream (page 45).

FRUIT PLATTER

Preparation time: 30 to 40 minutes

Yield: 8 to 10 servings

8 to 20 seasonal fruits of choice

▶ Cut the fruits into attractive shapes or bite-size pieces and arrange them on a platter. Cover and store in the refrigerator for up to 4 hours before serving.

GOJI-ORANGE SAUCE

Preparation time: 5 minutes (plus advance soaking time)   **Yield:** 8 to 10 servings (2½ cups)

The brilliant orange-red color of this sauce will excite guests of all ages and tempt them to try it.

1½ cups goji berries

1 cup freshly squeezed orange juice

▶ Combine the goji berries and orange juice in a bowl and let soak in the refrigerator for 2 to 4 hours. Transfer the fruit and juice to a blender and process until smooth. Refrigerate for at least 1 hour before serving to allow the sauce to thicken.

NOTE: If you don't have goji berries but would still like a colorful sauce, use Berry Dressing (page 49) instead of Goji-Orange Sauce.

CHOCOLATE-ORANGE SAUCE

Preparation time: 5 minutes   **Yield:** 8 to 10 servings (2¼ cups)

This is a velvety sauce that everyone will adore. It is the perfect chocolate dip and is easier to digest than one made with nuts.

1 cup freshly squeezed orange juice

½ cup raw cocoa powder

½ cup coconut oil

¼ cup agave syrup, or 4 pitted Medjool dates

▶ Combine all of the ingredients in a blender and process until smooth. Refrigerate for at least 1 hour before serving to allow the sauce to thicken.

Vegetable Platter with Savory Dips

Preparation time: 35 minutes   **Yield:** 8 to 10 servings

The trick with a vegetable platter is to choose your vegetables well and artfully arrange them without fussing too much. For the most visual excitement, use at least five different vegetables with a range of shapes and colors. Have fun and surprise your guests with some foods they may not have tried before. For example, jicama is a Mexican root vegetable that tastes like a cross between a potato and an apple with a hint of snow pea. It's a delicious, pure white addition to a vegetable platter and widely available at Asian grocery stores, natural food stores, and many mainstream supermarkets. Other good choices are snow peas, carrot sticks, colorful bell pepper strips, celery sticks, zucchini slices, whole green beans, daikon radish rounds, whole red radishes, and asparagus spears. Present your vegetable platter with one or two of the savory dips that follow.

VEGETABLE PLATTER

Preparation time: 30 to 40 minutes   **Yield:** 8 to 10 servings

8 to 10 cups vegetables of choice

▶ Cut large vegetables into appealing shapes or bite-size pieces. Green beans, snow peas, asparagus spears, cherry tomatoes, red radishes, and baby vegetables can be served whole. Arrange the prepared vegetables on an attractive platter. Cover and store in the refrigerator for up to 4 hours before serving. Offer cocktail napkins and a small glass of toothpicks when serving the platter, if desired.

TOMATO AND OLIVE TAPENADE

Preparation time: 20 minutes

Yield: 8 to 10 servings (2 to 3 cups)

1 large ripe tomato, finely chopped

1 red bell pepper, finely chopped

½ cup pitted olives (preferably kalamata), finely chopped

½ small red onion, finely chopped

1 tablespoon freshly squeezed lemon juice

1 clove garlic, finely chopped

Here is a quick and easy dish that complements any hors d'oeuvre table. Although it makes an excellent dip for a vegetable platter, you can also use it as a salad dressing or as a pâté to spread on crackers or vegetable slices. The best olives for this recipe are strong-flavored dark ones like kalamata.

▶ Combine all of the ingredients in a bowl and mix well. Serve immediately or cover and refrigerate for up to 1 day.

PISTACHIO PESTO

Preparation time: 15 minutes

Yield: 8 to 10 servings (about 1 cup)

1 cup fresh basil leaves

1 cup arugula

½ cup shelled raw pistachio nuts

⅓ cup extra-virgin olive oil

2 tablespoons freshly squeezed lemon juice

1 teaspoon sea salt

1 teaspoon lemon zest

This is an intriguing alternative to standard pesto; the secret ingredient is arugula, also known as rocket, which adds extra bite. Pesto loses some of its magic if it is turned into a purée, so be sure to keep the texture chunky.

▶ Combine all of the ingredients in a food processor fitted with the S blade and process until well mixed but still chunky.

VARIATION: Replace the pistachios with ½ cup raw cashews, macadamia nuts, or pine nuts.

NOTE: If you are making the pesto ahead of time, sprinkle a bit of lemon juice or extra-virgin olive oil on the surface to keep the color from darkening.

PÂTÉ DU SOLEIL

Preparation time: 40 minutes (plus advance soaking and sprouting time)   **Yield:** 8 to 10 servings (8 cups)

This is a versatile recipe that will keep for up to a week in the refrigerator. You can use it three different ways: in a roll-up, as a canapé, and as a dip. Serve it one way or try all three at your event.

3 cups raw sunflower seeds

1 large red bell pepper, coarsely chopped

¾ cup freshly squeezed lemon juice

½ cup raw tahini

½ cup coarsely chopped fresh parsley

½ small onion, coarsely chopped

4 green onions, coarsely chopped

2 tablespoons Nama Shoyu

2 to 3 cloves garlic, crushed

½ teaspoon cayenne

▶ Soak the sunflower seeds in water to cover plus 4 inches for 8 to 12 hours. Drain, rinse well, and drain again. Return the seeds to the bowl used for soaking them and let them rest at room temperature for 2 to 4 hours. After 4 hours, if you are not ready to continue with the recipe, transfer the seeds to a covered container and refrigerate to slow the sprouting process. Rinse and drain the seeds again, removing any husks that float to the surface. (The easiest way to remove the husks is to place the seeds in a large bowl filled with water several inches above the seeds. Swirl the seeds around with your hand and the husks will rise to the top for a few moments. Pour them off and repeat the process until you have discarded most of the husks.)

Combine all of the ingredients in a food processor fitted with the S blade and process until quite smooth. Taste and adjust the seasonings if necessary. Cover and store in the refrigerator until serving time. The garlic flavor will develop and become stronger in a few hours.

Variations

- For an Asian-flavored alternative, omit the lemon juice and add 1 cup of Japanese Shoyu Dressing (page 64).
- To vary the flavor and texture of the finished pâté, stir in ½ cup of your choice of the following options (use one or use a combination): chopped onion, minced fresh parsley or cilantro, minced celery, minced red bell pepper, chopped snow peas, chopped shallots.

Notes

- If you have a small food processor you may need to process the pâté in batches.
- This pâté can also be made with nuts or a combination of seeds and nuts; however, it will keep longer when made with sunflower seeds.

JAPANESE SHOYU DRESSING

See photo facing page 87.   **Preparation time:** 5 minutes   **Yield:** 24 to 30 servings (about 3 cups)

1 cup water

½ cup Nama Shoyu

6 tablespoons raw tahini

6 green onions, coarsely
chopped

3 to 4 tablespoons raw
honey or agave syrup

3 tablespoons flaxseed oil

3 tablespoons raw or
toasted sesame oil

3 tablespoons grated
 fresh ginger

2 to 3 cloves garlic,
crushed

¾ teaspoon Chinese
five-spice powder

½ teaspoon cayenne

½ teaspoon ground cumin

This is a light, thin dipping sauce or dressing. To add an Asian flair, use it as a flavorful replacement for lemon juice in savory recipes, nut loaves, or pâtés.

▶ Combine all of the ingredients in a blender and process until smooth. Taste and adjust the seasonings if necessary. Stored in a covered container in the refrigerator, Japanese Shoyu Dressing will keep for 2 to 3 weeks.

Save Steps with a High-Performance Blender!

If you have a high-performance blender, it is not necessary to crush garlic, grate ginger, or chop scallions prior to blending them. These steps are only necessary when using a regular home blender. Because of its superior power, a high-performance blender will pulverize whole garlic cloves, fresh ginger, and scallions without any advance work.

Zucchini Roll-Ups

Preparation time: 20 minutes (plus up to 36 hours dehydrating time)   **Yield:** 8 to 10 servings

These roll-ups are so delicious it will be hard to keep your guests from eating too many. This recipe is pictured between pages 86 and 87.

4 to 5 zucchini, at room temperature

2 to 3 cups Pâté du Soleil (page 63)

▶ Slice the zucchini lengthwise as thinly as possible using a mandoline on the thinnest setting or a very sharp knife.

Spread a ¼-inch-thick layer (or more, if desired) of the pâté on each zucchini slice and arrange in a single layer on mesh dehydrator trays. Dehydrate at 105 to 115 degrees F for 2 to 4 hours (the zucchini should be soft and flexible). Remove from the dehydrator and roll up each zucchini slice starting from the narrow end. If necessary, use a toothpick to hold the rolls together.

Remove every other dehydrator tray so the roll-ups will fit into the dehydrator. Dehydrate at 105 to 115 degrees F for 18 to 36 hours, or until the roll-ups are completely dry. Cool and store in an airtight container for up to 1 week.

Zucchini Canapés

Preparation time: 20 minutes   **Yield:** 8 to 10 servings (30 to 40 canapés)

4 to 5 zucchini

2 to 3 cups Pâté du Soleil (page 63)

Decorations of choice (such as sliced olives, finely diced colorful bell peppers, sliced onion, minced parsley or cilantro, edible flowers)

Make these canapés instead of Zucchini Roll-Ups (above) if you don't have a dehydrator. Top them with your favorite edible decorations—let your creativity go wild!

▶ Slice the zucchini into ¼-inch-thick rounds. Spread a ¼-inch-thick layer of the pâté on each round and arrange the rounds on an attractive serving platter. Top with the decorations of your choice.

TRADITIONAL

Menu

Stuffing

Marinated Mushrooms

Wilted Greens

Faux Mashed Potatoes with Mushroom Gravy

Sweet Potato Soufflé

Festive Loaf

Cranberry Sauce

Yam Pie or Applesauce Pie (choose one)

Equipment Needed

blender

citrus juicer or reamer

dehydrator (optional)

food processor

juicer (optional)

Traditional Menu

This is an easy and stress-free meal for the host because most of the dishes can be made at least one day in advance. There are many components to this meal, so your guests will need only a small amount of each dish.

This menu is considered "traditional" because it is in the style of a North American Thanksgiving or Christmas dinner. Some familiar foods are included: yams, cranberries, gravy, faux mashed potatoes, and stuffing. Just as important as the foods are the seasonings used; you can alter the character of a dish simply by changing the herbs and spices. Parsley, sage, rosemary, and thyme are the traditional flavors incorporated into this menu. Tasting them will evoke happy memories for anyone who has experienced a North American holiday meal.

Two to three weeks before your event:

■ make and freeze Yam Pie (page 80)

Four days before your event:

■ make Marinated Mushrooms (page 72)

Two days before your event:

■ do all of your grocery shopping

■ make Cranberry Sauce (page 78)

■ make Applesauce Pie (page 79)

One day before your event:

■ make Wilted Greens (page 73)

■ make Sweet Potato Soufflé (page 76)

■ make Stuffing (page 71)

■ make Festive Loaf (page 77)

■ make Mushroom Gravy (page 75)

■ set out serving dishes, flatware, and tablecloths

The day of your event:

■ make Faux Mashed Potatoes (page 74)

Stuffing

Zucchini absorbs the flavors of the herbs and seasonings and makes for a lighter stuffing. This recipe tastes best when it is made several hours before it is served so the flavors can mingle. If you don't have fresh herbs on hand, add poultry seasoning to taste, as it contains herbs and seasonings that are similar to those used in this recipe.

1 cup raw walnuts

1 cup raw macadamia nuts

1 cup peeled and coarsely chopped zucchini

1 small white onion, coarsely chopped

3 stalks celery, peeled (optional) and coarsely chopped

3 tablespoons fresh thyme

2 tablespoons fresh sage

1 teaspoon fresh rosemary

2 cloves garlic, minced

½ teaspoon freshly ground black pepper

½ teaspoon sea salt

▶ Place all of the ingredients in a food processor fitted with the S blade and process until coarsely chopped and well combined. Cover and refrigerate for 1 to 24 hours. If desired, dehydrate at 105 to 115 degrees F for 1 to 2 hours before serving to warm and soften the mixture, taking care that it doesn't dry out.

Marinated Mushrooms

See photo between pages 86 and 87. **Preparation time:** 45 minutes **Yield:** 8 to 10 servings

Prepare this dish one to four days in advance. Keep it tightly covered in the refrigerator and toss the ingredients once a day. If you make it the same day it will be served, allow at least two hours for it to marinate at room temperature and toss the ingredients often.

8 portobello mushrooms

½ cup extra-virgin olive oil

2 green onions, thinly sliced

¼ cup minced fresh parsley

3 tablespoons freshly squeezed lemon juice or apple cider vinegar

2 tablespoons finely minced onion

2 tablespoons Nama Shoyu

2 cloves garlic, finely minced or crushed

1 teaspoon sea salt

▶ Remove the stems and gills (see note) from the mushrooms and wipe the caps clean with a damp cloth or paper towel. Cut each mushroom cap in half, then thinly slice it. Place all of the remaining ingredients in a shallow bowl, add the mushroom slices, and gently toss until they are evenly coated. Let marinate at room temperature for 1 hour. Cover and refrigerate, tossing occasionally. Bring to room temperature before serving.

NOTE: Mushroom gills can be easily removed with the tip of a teaspoon.

Wilted Greens

Preparation time: 15 minutes (plus time for greens to soften)

Yield: 8 to 10 servings

This recipe calls for the type of greens that are typically cooked, such as collard, beet, dandelion, kale, mustard, turnip, and Swiss chard leaves. Choose leafy vegetables that are thicker and more robust than delicate greens like romaine lettuce or spinach. For greens that are pungent, like mustard and dandelion, a little sweetener in the dressing helps soften their strong taste. For greens that are hardy but not pungent, a salty and savory flavoring works well.

25 to 30 large, hardy, dark green vegetable leaves

1 to 2 teaspoons sea salt, Herbamare, or Trocomare

1 to 2 teaspoons agave syrup, date sugar, or maple sugar (use for pungent greens only, such as mustard greens)

1 to 2 tablespoons freshly squeezed lemon juice (use for less pungent greens only, such as Swiss chard)

2 tablespoons walnut oil or extra-virgin olive oil

Wash and dry the greens and cut out any hard stems. Arrange the leaves in stacks, using 4 to 5 leaves per stack. Roll up each stack tightly like a cigar, then thinly slice the rolls crosswise into strips (this is known as chiffonade). Place the strips in a bowl and sprinkle them with the sea salt. Toss the greens and massage and squeeze them with your hands for several minutes until they soften and begin to get juicy.

Add either agave syrup or lemon juice, depending on how pungent or mild the greens are, and toss thoroughly. Let rest at room temperature for 1 to 3 hours to soften and develop some liquid. If time is limited, toss and massage the greens gently with a wooden spoon every few minutes; they will be ready in 10 to 15 minutes. Just before serving, add the oil and toss. Taste and adjust the seasonings, if necessary.

Faux Mashed Potatoes

Preparation time: 25 minutes (plus advance soaking time)

Yield: 8 to 10 servings (8 cups)

This recipe is our adaptation of one made famous by Juliano, author of *Raw: The Uncook Book*. It tastes like the real thing, especially when smothered with our Mushroom Gravy (page 75). Make this recipe the day of your event.

1½ cups raw cashews, soaked for 20 minutes

1 medium cauliflower, chopped (about 6 cups)

½ cup freshly squeezed lemon juice or fresh celery juice

2 tablespoons extra-virgin olive oil or flaxseed oil

½ teaspoon sea salt

2 tablespoons dehydrated vegetables (optional)

▶ Drain the cashews, rinse well, and drain again. Place in a blender along with the cauliflower, ¼ cup of the lemon juice, and all of the oil and salt. Process until completely smooth, adding a small amount of additional juice as needed to facilitate processing. Stir in the optional dehydrated vegetables and let rest for 30 to 60 minutes to allow the dehydrated vegetables to absorb some of the moisture and soften.

VARIATION: Replace half of the cauliflower with 3 cups of peeled and chopped parsnips. The parsnips will mellow the flavor of the cauliflower and add a delicate, buttery color.

NOTE: If you don't have a high-performance blender, you can make this recipe in a food processor fitted with the S blade. Although it will taste delicious, it won't be as smooth and creamy. Alternatively, you can process the cauliflower and cashews through a heavy-duty juicer using the blank screen, then transfer the mixture to a food processor fitted with the S blade or a regular home blender and process until smooth.

Mushroom Gravy

Preparation time: 10 minutes   **Yield:** 6 to 8 servings (1¼ cups)

This popular recipe was first featured in Nomi's book *The Raw Gourmet*. Be sure to have enough ingredients on hand in case you want to make a double batch. If you like, the gravy can be gently warmed over very low heat on the stovetop before serving. It also doubles as a delicious soup!

2½ cups quartered cremini mushrooms

½ cup water

¼ cup raw almond butter

1 tablespoon minced onion

2 teaspoons Nama Shoyu

Pinch of sea salt

▶ Combine all of the ingredients in a blender and process until smooth. Use about 2 tablespoons of gravy for each serving of Faux Mashed Potatoes (page 74).

Sweet Potato Soufflé

Preparation time: 30 minutes

Yield: 5 to 6 cups

This is a very sweet side dish that contrasts well with all the savory tastes on the menu. Look for yams or sweet potatoes with very deep orange flesh. Garnet and jewel yams are highly recommended.

This recipe was adapted from the Raw Soul Food recipe collection of Lynda Carter at aliveandraw.com.

4 large yams or sweet potatoes

3 tablespoons freshly squeezed lemon juice, or 1 teaspoon lemon extract

1 cup water, more or less as needed

½ cup raw cashews

½ cup raw pine nuts or macadamia nuts

2 vanilla beans, or 2 teaspoons vanilla extract

6 to 8 pitted dates

1 tablespoon ground cinnamon

¼ teaspoon grated nutmeg

▶ Peel the yams and cut them into small cubes. Transfer to a blender along with the lemon juice and enough water to allow the blender to work properly. Process until thick and chunky. Add the remaining ingredients and process until smooth and creamy. Add more water, 1 tablespoon at a time, only if necessary to facilitate processing.

Festive Loaf

Preparation time: 20 minutes

Yield: 8 small servings (1 loaf)

T his is a rich and hearty loaf, lightened with chopped fresh vegetables and savory herbs. Make it one day before your event to allow the flavors to develop.

LOAF

1 cup raw cashews

1 cup raw pecans

1 red bell pepper, chopped

3 stalks celery, finely chopped

2 shallots, chopped

1 tablespoon fresh rosemary

½ small red onion, finely chopped

1 tablespoon finely chopped fresh parsley

3 tablespoons Cranberry Sauce (optional; page 78)

BREADING

3 tablespoons ground flaxseeds

2 tablespoons dulse powder

Pinch of cayenne

¼ cup raw pecans

Parsley sprigs

▶ **FOR THE LOAF,** combine the cashews, pecans, red bell pepper, two-thirds of the celery, and all of the shallots and rosemary in a food processor fitted with the S blade and process until smooth. Stir in the onion, the remaining celery, and the parsley. For a marbled effect, lightly swirl in the optional Cranberry Sauce. Place on a serving platter and form into a loaf.

▶ **FOR THE BREADING,** combine the flaxseeds, dulse, and cayenne in a bowl and sprinkle over the top and sides of the loaf, pressing it on gently. Decorate the top of the loaf with the whole pecans and a few parsley sprigs. Refrigerate for at least 24 hours before serving. This will allow the flavors to blend and the loaf to firm up.

Cranberry Sauce

See photo between pages 86 and 87.   **Preparation time:** 20 minutes   **Yield:** 8 to 10 servings (about 3 cups)

Cranberries need plenty of added sweetness to mellow their tartness; for this we rely on wholesome dates and juicy oranges. This is an amazingly simple recipe to prepare, and it is always a big hit, even with those who are used to more conventional holiday fare. Another bonus is that it can be made two to three days in advance.

1 teaspoon orange zest (optional)

1 to 2 oranges

1 package (12 ounces) fresh cranberries, rinsed well and drained

4 pitted dates, or more as needed

▶ If using, remove the orange zest before juicing the oranges. Transfer the orange zest, orange juice, and all of the remaining ingredients to a blender and process just until chunky. Taste and blend in more dates, one at a time, if additional sweetness is needed.

NOTE: If you prefer, an equal amount of frozen cranberries may be used instead of fresh cranberries. Thaw them before processing.

Applesauce Pie

Preparation time: 40 minutes

Yield: 8 to 10 servings

Rich, sweet, and fragrant with cinnamon, this pie is a good choice to offer your most skeptical friends—they'll never guess it wasn't baked! Use two or three varieties of apples for a uniform flavor that's not too tart or sweet. For maximum nutrition, color, and fiber, do not peel the apples.

CRUST

1¼ cups raw almonds, pecans, or walnuts, soaked for 10 to 12 hours

1 cup chopped dates

1 tablespoon water

½ teaspoon vanilla extract

Pinch of ground cinnamon

2 teaspoons psyllium powder

FILLING

10 apples, coarsely chopped

2 cups pitted dates, as needed

1 cup raisins

1 tablespoon freshly squeezed lemon juice

3 tablespoons psyllium powder

Apple slices dipped in lemon juice

▶ **FOR THE CRUST,** drain the almonds, rinse well, and drain again. Transfer the almonds to a food processor fitted with the S blade and process into a coarse meal. Add the dates and process until they are finely ground. With the machine running, gradually add the water, vanilla extract, and cinnamon through the opening in the lid. When the crust starts to hold together, add the psyllium powder and process just until it is evenly incorporated. Immediately press the mixture evenly into the bottom and up the sides of an 8- or 9-inch pie pan.

▶ **FOR THE FILLING,** combine the chopped apples, 1 cup of the dates, and all of the raisins and lemon juice in a high-performance blender or a food processor fitted with the S blade. Process until smooth, stopping to scrape down the sides of the container as necessary. Taste and add additional dates to achieve the desired sweetness. Add the cinnamon and process until evenly distributed. With the machine running, slowly add the psyllium powder through the opening in the lid. Immediately pour the filling into the crust. Decorate the top with thinly sliced apples that have been dipped in lemon juice so they won't brown. Cover and refrigerate.

NOTE: If you don't have psyllium powder, make the recipe in individual ramekins so the pie doesn't have to be sliced.

Yam Pie

See photo between pages 86 and 87.   **Preparation time:** 1 hour (plus advance soaking time)   **Yield:** 8 to 10 servings

Y ou might be wondering why we include a dessert with yams since yams are also part of the main meal. The answer is that holiday meals often contain many complex dishes, which can lead to digestive discomfort. To help prevent this, it is better to limit the variety of foods served at a meal and make as many dishes as possible from the same basic ingredients. The most appreciated feature of Yam Pie (besides its delicious taste) is that it can be made far in advance of an event and successfully frozen. Few raw food recipes freeze well, so if planning ahead is what you need to do, this pie will fit right in with your schedule.

CRUST

1¼ cup raw almonds, walnuts, or pecans, soaked for 8 to 12 hours

1 cup chopped dates

1 tablespoon water

1 teaspoon vanilla extract (optional)

¼ teaspoon ground cinnamon

2 teaspoons psyllium powder

▶ **FOR THE CRUST,** drain the almonds, rinse well, drain again, and dry them in clean kitchen towels. Transfer the almonds to a food processor fitted with the S blade and pulse until they are coarsely but evenly chopped. Add the dates and process until the almonds are finely ground. With the machine running, gradually add the water, optional vanilla extract, and cinnamon through the opening in the lid. The crust should hold together when pinched between your fingers. If it does not, add a small amount of additional water, about 1/2 teaspoon at a time, until it does. Gradually add the psyllium powder and process until it is evenly incorporated. Immediately press the mixture into an 8- or 9-inch pie pan. Use the crust as is or dehydrate it at 105 to 115 degrees F for 1 to 2 hours.

FILLING

1 teaspoon orange zest

1 orange

¼ cup raisins

¾ cup pitted dates, soaked for 20 minutes

6 small yams (orange flesh or a mix of orange and white flesh)

1 teaspoon vanilla extract, or 1 vanilla bean, ground in a spice grinder or coffee grinder

½ cup raw pine nuts

¾ teaspoon ground cinnamon

¼ teaspoon sea salt

¼ teaspoon Chinese 5-spice powder

⅛ teaspoon ground cloves

⅛ teaspoon garam masala or additional Chinese 5-spice powder

2 tablespoons psyllium powder

▶ **FOR THE FILLING,** remove the orange zest and set it aside. Juice the orange and place the juice in a bowl. Add the raisins and let soak for 20 minutes.

Drain the dates and reserve the soaking water. Drain the raisins and reserve the orange juice. Peel the yams and cut them into chunks. Combine the yams, orange juice, reserved orange zest, and vanilla extract in a high-performance blender and process until smooth. Add some of the date soaking water if necessary to facilitate blending. Add the dates, raisins, pine nuts, cinnamon, salt, Chinese 5-spice powder, cloves, and garam masala and process until smooth. Add a small amount more of the date soaking water only if necessary to facilitate blending. Taste and adjust the seasonings if necessary. Gradually blend in the psyllium powder.

Immediately pour the filling into the prepared crust, cover, and refrigerate if using soon. Alternatively, freeze the pie and transfer to the refrigerator to thaw 1 day before your event.

VARIATION: If you like, top each serving with a dollop of Cashew Cream (page 45) or pass a pitcher of Cashew Cream at the table.

NOTE: If you do not have a high-performance blender, use a heavy-duty juicer with a blank screen. Process the yams, dates, raisins, and pine nuts through the juicer. Transfer to a food processor fitted with the S blade and add the orange juice, reserved orange zest, pine nuts, vanilla extract, cinnamon, salt, Chinese 5-spice powder, cloves, and garam masala and process until smooth. Add a small amount of the date soaking water only if necessary to facilitate processing. When the mixture is smooth, taste and adjust the seasonings if necessary. Gradually add the psyllium powder and process until evenly incorporated. Pour into the prepared crust as directed.

LIGHT LUNCH

Menu

Equipment Needed

blender

citrus juicer or reamer

dehydrator (optional)

food processor

mandoline (optional)

Light Luncheon Buffet

This menu is a bit different from the others, as it includes several recipes found elsewhere in the book. We did this intentionally so you can practice mixing and matching recipes and ideas that go beyond a set theme to create your own variations.

This menu is designed to be served as a buffet, although you could just as easily serve it as a sit-down meal if you prefer. Starting with fresh fruit is always an excellent idea, as it aids digestion and allows everyone to thoroughly enjoy the first course. Surprise your guests with exotic fruits that will tickle their taste buds.

Five to six days before your event:

- make either Luscious Lemon Cookies (page 92) or Orange-Coconut Biscotti (page 93) using a dehydrator

Four to five days before your event:

- do all of your grocery shopping
- make Marinated Mushrooms (page 72)

Three days before your event:

- make Japanese Shoyu Dressing (page 64)

Two days before your event:

- make Sweet Citrus Dressing (page 91)
- wash and dry salad greens for Summer Salad with Japanese Shoyu Dressing (page 87)

One day before your event:

- make Dilled Spinach Mousse (page 88)
- make Creamy Dill Sauce (page 90)
- make Luscious Lemon Cookies (page 92), if not using a dehydrator
- set out serving dishes, flatware, and tablecloths

Day of your event:

- make Julienned Vegetables with Sweet Citrus Dressing (page 91)
- make Fresh Seasonal Fruit (page 87)
- toss the salad with the dressing just before serving or serve the dressing on the side

Berry Dressing, p. 49

Apple-Cranberry Tart, p. 51

Fruit Platter, p. 59

Zucchini Roll-Ups, p. 65

Cranberry Sauce, p. 78

Marinated Mushrooms, p. 72

Yam Pie, p. 80

Summer Salad, p. 87, with Japanese Shoyu Dressing, p. 64

Fresh Seasonal Fruit

Preparation time: varies   **Yield:** 8 to 10 servings

Simple fruit dishes are a great opportunity to experiment with creative presentations and let your imagination run wild. There are several options you can choose for your fruit course. Plan on one to two whole fruits per person, depending on what else you are serving.

Consider Fruit Kabobs (page 50) or Platter of Seasonal Fruits (page 49) with Berry Dressing (page 49). Alternatively, try your hand at carving a watermelon basket and fill it with a mixture of watermelon, cantaloupe, honeydew, and/or other melons and fruit cut into bite-size pieces. A pineapple also makes a lovely serving basket. Cut the pineapple in half lengthwise (keep the leaves intact). Scoop out the flesh and cut it into bite-size pieces. Then fill both halves with the pineapple chunks and assorted seasonal fruits. Lay the halves end to end for an impressive display.

Summer Salad with Japanese Shoyu Dressing

See photo, facing page.   **Preparation time:** 10 minutes   **Yield:** 8 to 10 servings

10 to 20 cups baby salad greens or other salad greens of your choice

2 surprise ingredients (see sidebar, page 111)

1 cup Japanese Shoyu Dressing (page 64), more or less as needed

Baby greens and a light, tasty dressing make an exceptional combination. Surprise your guests with a crunchy addition that contrasts with the tender texture of the greens.

▶ Combine the greens and surprise ingredients and toss gently. Add the dressing and toss just before serving. Alternatively, serve the dressing on the side or pass it at the table.

Dilled Spinach Mousse

Preparation time: 1 hour (plus advance soaking time)   **Yield:** 8 servings

This recipe can be made one day in advance. For a lighter dish, the mousse can be prepared without the crust. This is a delicately flavored recipe, so take care not to overwhelm it with strong flavors like onion or garlic. It is intended to be mild and pleasantly bland, similar to a spinach quiche with a hint of nutmeg. The psyllium powder is essential, as otherwise the mousse will be too soft to slice. If you cannot find psyllium powder, use individual ramekins rather than a pie pan so it won't need to be sliced; although the mousse will have a slightly different texture, your guests won't know the difference and it will still taste delicious.

We recommend using mild-flavored white button mushrooms so they don't overpower the dish. The mushrooms should be more of a background taste. Serve the mousse with Creamy Dill Sauce.

CRUST

2 to 3 cups raw almonds, soaked 8 to 12 hours

1 tablespoon Nama Shoyu, or a pinch of sea salt

2 to 4 tablespoons water

2 tablespoons psyllium powder

FOR THE CRUST, drain the almonds, rinse well, and drain again. Dry the almonds using a clean kitchen towel or place them in the sun or in a dehydrator at 105 to 115 degrees F for about 1 hour. Transfer the almonds to a food processor fitted with the S blade and process until uniformly chopped. Add the Nama Shoyu and pulse until it is evenly distributed. Add the water 1 tablespoon at a time and process just until the mixture holds together. With the processor running, gradually add the psyllium powder through the opening in the lid and process until evenly distributed. Press the mixture into a 9-inch pie pan. For a crisp texture, place the crust in the sun for 1 to 2 hours, or dehydrate it at 105 to 115 degrees F for 30 to 60 minutes.

FILLING

1 pound spinach

3 cups sliced white button mushrooms, including the trimmed stems

4 tablespoons raw tahini

4 tablespoons coarsely chopped fresh dill

3 tablespoons freshly squeezed lemon or lime juice

2 tablespoons raw pine nuts

¾ teaspoon sea salt

1/8 teaspoon grated nutmeg

5 tablespoons water, or more as needed

2 tablespoons psyllium powder

DECORATIONS
(optional)

Fresh herbs

Thinly sliced mushrooms

Walnuts

FOR THE FILLING, clean and dry the spinach and tear it into pieces. Alternatively, use prewashed baby spinach. Place the spinach, mushrooms, tahini, dill, lemon juice, pine nuts, salt, and nutmeg in a food processor fitted with the S blade and process until smooth and evenly green. Add the water, 1 tablespoon at a time, as necessary to facilitate processing and achieve a smooth consistency. With the machine running, gradually add the psyllium powder through the opening in the lid and process until evenly distributed. Immediately press the filling into the pie crust (or directly into a pie pan or ramekins if not using a crust). Refrigerate for at least 1 hour before serving to allow the mousse to firm up.

Garnish the chilled mousse with the optional decorations of your choice.

Variations

- Replace the spinach with 1 pound of broccoli florets, coarsely chopped.
- For a large crowd, omit the crust, make several batches of the mousse, put it in a large rectangular pan, and cut it in squares to serve.

Creamy Dill Sauce

Preparation Time: 10 minutes (plus advance soaking time)　　　　　**Yield:** 2½ cups

This creamy dressing looks beautiful on Dilled Spinach Mousse (page 88), as it provides the perfect contrast. The dill is chopped, not blended, so the color of the sauce remains light with tiny flecks of dill throughout. The sauce can be made one or two days prior to your event.

½ cup raw macadamia nuts, soaked for 20 minutes

½ cup raw cashews, soaked for 20 minutes

1 cup water

½ teaspoon sea salt (optional)

2 tablespoons freshly squeezed lemon juice

½ cup coarsely chopped fresh dill

▶ Drain the macadamia nuts and cashews, rinse well, and drain again. Transfer the nuts to a blender, add the water and optional salt, and process until smooth. Add the lemon juice and blend again briefly. Pour into a bowl and stir in the dill. Refrigerate for at least 2 hours before serving. The sauce will thicken as it chills.

Julienned Vegetables with Sweet Citrus Dressing

Preparation time: 20 to 40 minutes

Yield: 8 servings

his dish can be made several hours in advance and looks very attractive next to the green Dilled Spinach Mousse.

JULIENNED VEGETABLES

6 carrots, julienned

3 medium to large zucchini, julienned

3 red bell peppers, julienned

▶ **FOR THE VEGETABLES,** put the carrots, zucchini, and peppers into a large bowl and toss until well combined.

NOTE: Although you can julienne the carrots and zucchini by hand using a sharp knife, it will be faster and easier if you use a mandoline. If you don't have access to a mandoline, cut the vegetables into 3- to 4-inch-long matchsticks. It is best to julienne the peppers by hand.

SWEET CITRUS DRESSING

Preparation time: 10 minutes

Yield: 1½ cups

2 teaspoons orange zest

1 cup freshly squeezed orange juice

¼ cup raw tahini

2 tablespoons freshly squeezed lemon or lime juice

2 teaspoons dulse flakes

2 teaspoons grated fresh ginger

½ teaspoon ground cinnamon

¼ teaspoon curry powder

¼ teaspoon sea salt

▶ Remove the orange zest before juicing the oranges. Transfer the orange zest, orange juice, and all of the remaining ingredients to a blender and process until smooth. Pour over the julienned vegetables and toss until evenly coated. Let marinate for 1 to 2 hours in the refrigerator before serving.

Luscious Lemon Cookies

Preparation time: 30 minutes (plus optional dehydrating time)   **Yield:** about 16 cookies

These cookies were originally developed to be dehydrated, but everyone who has tried them fresh agrees they taste great just as they are, so you can make them either way. If you are not dehydrating the cookies, use dried coconut rather than fresh for the best results.

¼ cup lemon zest

¾ cup freshly squeezed lemon juice

2 cups raw cashews

2 cups shredded mature fresh coconut or unsweetened shredded dried coconut

¼ cup agave syrup or other sweetener of choice

½ to 1 teaspoon lemon extract (optional)

▶ Remove the lemon zest before juicing the lemons. Transfer the lemon zest, lemon juice, and all of the remaining ingredients to a blender and process until smooth. Shape into cookies and place on mesh dehydrator sheets. Dehydrate at 105 to 115 degrees F until for 8 to 10 hours, or until the outside is dry and the cookie is chewy.

NOTE: A high-performance blender is the best choice to use with this recipe. If you are using a regular home blender, grind the cashews finely (in an electric coffee grinder, dry blender, or food processor fitted with the S blade) before processing them with the other ingredients.

Orange-Coconut Biscotti

Preparation time: 30 minutes (plus dehydrating time)

Yield: about 16 cookies

These cookies are a fabulous way to use up extra coconut or almond pulp. They need to be fully dehydrated to get the crunch associated with biscotti; you will be amazed at the texture. You can get coconut pulp by making coconut milk (see pages 32 and 58).

1 teaspoon orange zest

2 oranges, juiced

1 lemon, juiced

½ cup raw cashews

3 cups fresh coconut pulp

4 tablespoons agave syrup

1 teaspoon ground cinnamon

▶ Remove the orange zest before juicing the oranges and set it aside. Combine the orange juice, lemon juice, and cashews in a blender and process until smooth. Transfer to a food processor fitted with the S blade. Add the coconut pulp, reserved orange zest, agave syrup, and cinnamon and process until well combined. The mixture may seem loose and crumbly; it will hold together once it is dried. Shape the mixture into cookies and place on mesh dehydrator sheets. Dehydrate at 105 to 115 degrees F for 12 to 16 hours, or until completely dry and crisp.

VARIATION: For an interesting flavor with additional complexity, omit the agave syrup and use 2 tablespoons yacon syrup instead.

NOTE: For an attractive decoration, press a thin slice of orange into the top of each cookie before dehydrating.

The majority of ingredients used in the recipes in this book can be purchased locally at natural food stores, gourmet shops, farmers markets, or well-stocked supermarkets. If you live in a more rural or isolated area, you can order most of the ingredients through online retailers. Please see the Resources section (page 103) for a list of suppliers.

AGAVE SYRUP. Also known as agave nectar, agave syrup is a low-glycemic natural sweetener made from the same family of succulents used to make tequila. Not all agave syrup is raw. A number of manufacturers claim that their agave syrup is raw, but we are not completely sure about that. Check the label and buy from a brand you trust. Light agave syrup is similar in taste and color to mild honey; dark agave syrup is more strongly flavored.

ALMOND BUTTER. Similar in consistency to peanut butter, almond butter is a spread made from raw or toasted almonds. Raw almond butter is available at natural food stores and from online retailers. It can also be made at home by processing raw (unsoaked) almonds in a food processor fitted with the S blade until they form a smooth paste (a small amount of added oil may be required to obtain a smooth texture), or by running them through a heavy-duty juicer fitted with the blank plate.

APPLE CIDER VINEGAR. Raw apple cider vinegar is made from fermented apple cider.

BALSAMIC VINEGAR. This is a dark, rich vinegar. The best balsamics are made from white Trebbiano grapes and are aged in wooden casks for a minimum of 12 years. Balsamic vinegar is not available raw.

CAROB POWDER. Often used as a substitute for cocoa powder, carob powder is ground from the dried pulp of the pods from the carob tree. Carob is also known as St. John's bread and locust bean. Look for carob powder that is labeled "raw."

CHINESE FIVE-SPICE POWDER. Used extensively in Chinese cooking, five-spice powder is an aromatic blend of cinnamon, cloves, fennel seed, star anise, and Szechuan peppercorns. It lends an unmistakable Asian flavor to recipes.

COCOA BUTTER. Cocoa butter is the fat extracted from cacao beans during the process of making chocolate and cocoa powder. Solid at room temperature, cocoa butter can be melted in a bowl placed over hot water.

COCOA POWDER. Unsweetened cocoa powder is ground from dried cacao beans after their oil has been extracted. The official term is "cocoa powder," though in some circles it is referred to as "cacao."

COCONUT, MATURE. Mature coconuts are the brown-husked fruits found in most grocery stores. Their flesh is thick and rich. It's important to choose a coconut that sounds like there is water inside when it is shaken. If the water tastes sour, it means the coconut is spoiled.

COCONUT, YOUNG. Also called Thai coconuts and young Thai coconuts, young coconuts are usually found precut into a white cylinder with a pointed top. The flesh varies from creamy to rubbery, and the water is usually very tasty. Young coconuts can be found in most Asian grocery stores and occasionally in natural food stores and well-stocked supermarkets. They are very popular with raw food enthusiasts, who enjoy them plain or use them in recipes.

COCONUT MILK. This fluid is made by blending mature coconut meat with coconut water and straining out the pulp.

COCONUT OIL. Coconut oil is pressed from the flesh of mature coconuts. It is a naturally saturated fat comprised of medium-chain fatty acids, which are considered to be health promoting. When stored at temperatures under 75 degrees F coconut oil becomes solid; at temperatures above 75 degrees F it becomes liquid. It is usually referred to as "oil" when it is liquid and "butter" when it is solid.

CREMINI MUSHROOM. A dark brown variation of the common white mushroom, the cremini is an immature portobello mushroom. Also known as the common brown mushroom, it is firmer and more flavorful than its white counterpart.

CUMIN. Shaped like a caraway seed, cumin is a pungent spice that is popular in Asian, Mediterranean, Middle Eastern, and Indian cuisine. It is available whole or ground and can be found in the spice aisle of ethnic and mainstream grocery stores. Cumin is also used as a digestive aid.

CURRY POWDER. Widely used in Indian cuisine, curry powder is a complex blend of a variety of spices such as cardamom, chiles, cinnamon, cloves, coriander, cumin, fenugreek, and turmeric. The exact spices used can vary greatly among brands.

DATE SUGAR. Date sugar is made from ground, dehydrated dates. It is an alternative to refined sugar, but it does not dissolve. Although it is a natural product, date sugar is not a raw food.

DEHYDRATED VEGETABLES. Dehydrated vegetables, whether a mixture or just one kind, are useful to thicken sauces and add flavor.

DULSE. A type of sea vegetable, dulse is reddish-brown in color with a delightful, salty flavor. Dulse is available in large pieces, flaked, or powdered.

FLAXSEEDS AND FLAXSEED OIL. Flaxseeds, also known as linseeds, are rich in omega-3 essential fatty acids. In raw cuisine, flaxseeds are commonly used as a thickener in recipes as well as a main ingredient in dehydrated crackers and cookies. Flaxseeds come in two colors: brown and golden. They can be used interchangeably, although the brown seeds tend to have a slightly stronger flavor and will add a brown tinge to recipes. Whole flaxseeds can be stored at room temperature. Ground flaxseeds should be made and used immediately. Flaxseed oil is pressed from whole raw flaxseeds. Store flaxseed oil in the refrigerator or freezer to ensure freshness, as it will go rancid quickly at room temperature. Flaxseeds are available at natural food stores and from online retailers. Look for flaxseed oil in the refrigerated section of your natural food store. We recommend Barlean's brand.

GALANGAL. A Southeast Asian relative of ginger, galangal is a light-colored rhizome that is popular in Thai cuisine. It has a unique, peppery flavor and is primarily used as a seasoning. Galangal is available at Asian markets and some natural food stores.

GARAM MASALA. There are many variations of garam masala, which is a traditional Indian seasoning blend that typically includes black pepper, cardamom, cinnamon, cloves, coriander, cumin, dried chiles, and other spices. Garam masala imparts warmth and an exotic flavor to food.

GOJI BERRIES. Also known as wolfberries, goji berries are small, almond-shaped, bright red berries traditionally grown in the Ningxiua region of Tibet. Because they are very rich in nutrients, including amino acids, antioxidants, carotenoids, vitamins, and minerals, goji berries have developed a reputation in the West as a superfood. They taste like a combination of raisins and dried cranberries.

HEMPSEED OIL. Hempseed oil is a nutritious, pale green oil extracted from the seeds of the hemp plant. It has a 3:1 ratio of omega-6 to omega-3 essential fatty acids. Store hempseed oil in the refrigerator or freezer to ensure freshness, as it will go rancid quickly at room temperature. Look for hempseed oil in the refrigerated section of your natural food store.

HERBAMARE. Containing a blend of sea salt and 14 organically grown herbs, Herbamare adds a flavorful seasoning boost to any savory dish. Look for Herbamare in the spice aisle of your natural food store.

ITALIAN SEASONING. A classic Italian seasoning blend contains a mixture of dried herbs such as basil, marjoram, oregano, rosemary, sage, and/or thyme.

KAFFIR LIME LEAVES. The glossy, dark green leaves of the kaffir lime tree, native to Southeast Asia and Hawaii, are a classic seasoning in Thai cuisine. They have a unique shape and unusual floral-citrus aroma. Look for kaffir lime leaves in Asian markets and gourmet shops. If you are unable to find them, use lime zest or freshly squeezed lime juice as an alternative. The fruit of kaffir limes is not edible, but the zest can be used as a substitute for the leaves.

KELP. Also known as kombu, kelp is the generic name for any of the large brown sea vegetables in the family Laminariaceae. It is a rich source of vitamins, minerals, and other nutrients. Kelp is available in large pieces or granules.

MAPLE SUGAR. Also known as maple granules or maple sprinkles, maple sugar is made from the boiled sap of the maple tree, which is cooked until the liquid has almost entirely evaporated.

MAPLE SYRUP. Although it is a natural product, maple syrup is not a raw food; it is the boiled sap of the maple tree. Maple syrup is very sweet, so a little goes a long way. Be sure to purchase only pure maple syrup, not pancake syrup, which is typically made from corn syrup and food coloring.

MISO. Miso is a thick, flavorful paste typically made from soybeans or other legumes, grain, and salt. It is used as a seasoning or salt replacement. There are many types of miso; generally the darker the color the stronger the flavor. Although not a raw product, naturally fermented, unpasteurized miso contains friendly bacteria and beneficial enzymes, making it very digestible. Be sure that any soy-based miso you purchase is certified organic, as virtually all nonorganic soybeans grown in North America are genetically modified. Look for miso in the refrigerated section of your natural food store.

NAMA SHOYU. Used as a salt substitute, Nama Shoyu is a naturally fermented, unpasteurized soy sauce that contains wheat. Although the manufacturer claims that it is raw, we cannot be certain this is true, so use it with discretion.

NORI. Commonly used to make sushi, nori is a popular sea vegetable that comes in square sheets. Nori is available raw (a purple-green color) or toasted (green).

NUTMEG. Nutmeg is the seed of the fruit of the nutmeg tree. Its flavor is warm, spicy, and sweet. Nutmeg is sold ground or whole. Whole nutmeg may be freshly ground with a fine grater; its flavor is superior to nutmeg that is commercially ground and packaged.

OATS. Soaked whole oat groats are sometimes used in raw food preparations. Although most oat groats have been steamed (often referred to as "stabilized"), raw oat groats are available at some natural food stores and from online retailers.

OLIVE OIL. For the best quality, buy only cold-pressed, extra-virgin olive oil. It should have a light, mild flavor. Store it in a dark pantry.

OLIVES, KALAMATA. The kalamata is an almond-shaped, rich, fruity-tasting Greek olive that is dark purple to brownish black in color. Kalamata olives are widely available at supermarkets and ethnic grocery stores. Raw and sun-dried kalamata olives can be purchased at natural food stores and from online retailers.

PÂTÉ. Raw pâtés are spreads, dips, or fillings usually made from nuts or seeds. Hummus is a traditional cooked pâté that is familiar to many people.

PINE NUTS. Also called pignoli, pignolia, and piñon, the pine nut is a soft white nut used primarily for sauces in raw cuisine. Due to their high oil content, pine nuts are best stored in the freezer.

PIZZA SEASONING. Pizza seasoning is a salt-free blend of popular Italian herbs. Our favorite brand is Frontier Herbs.

PORTOBELLO MUSHROOM. Portobello mushrooms are mature cremini mushrooms. Brown in color and rich in flavor, they are distinguished by their large, wide cap.

PSYLLIUM POWDER. Psyllium powder is made from the ground husks of psyllium seeds. The powder is used in raw cuisine as a thickener. Buy only finely ground psyllium powder with no additives, or grind the coarser husks at home in a blender.

SEA SALT. While no salt is health promoting, sea salt, Celtic salt, and Himalayan crystal salt are unrefined products that contain trace minerals. Use all salt and salty seasonings (like soy sauce, Nama Shoyu, and miso) in moderation.

SEASONED SALT. Unrefined salt blended with powdered dried vegetables is a great way to reduce sodium and add more flavor to dishes. Two of our favorite seasoned salts are Herbamare and Trocomare.

SESAME OIL. Sesame oil is pressed from raw or toasted sesame seeds. Raw sesame oil is light in color and taste. Toasted sesame oil is very dark with a rich flavor; small amounts are used as a seasoning.

SPROUTS. Most raw organic nuts, seeds, grains, and legumes can be sprouted or germinated after they have been soaked. Some are simply soaked and then rinsed, while others are soaked, rinsed, and then allowed to grow a short "tail." Still others are grown indoors in soil, such as sunflower, buckwheat, and pea sprouts. Sprouts are highly nutritious and easily digested.

SUN-DRIED TOMATOES. Dehydrating tomatoes concentrates their flavor and extends their shelf life indefinitely. We recommend using the dry, packaged tomatoes, not the ones packed in oil. Most recipes require soaking (rehydrating) sun-dried tomatoes in water before they are used. Most commercial sun-dried tomatoes are actually machine dehydrated, not sun dried. Dried tomatoes are easy to make at home if you own a dehydrator.

TAHINI. Tahini is a paste made from very finely ground sesame seeds. Similar to peanut butter in consistency, tahini is available raw or roasted. It is highly nutritious and economical, so it is used in many recipes.

TAMARI. Tamari is a naturally brewed soy sauce that is wheat free and may be used as a salt substitute. Tamari is not raw; for a raw alternative, use Nama Shoyu (see page 99).

THAI BASIL. Thai basil is a particular variety of sweet basil with a unique flavor that is popular in Thai and other Asian cuisines. If you cannot find fresh Thai bail, regular basil may be substituted.

VANILLA BEAN. Vanilla beans are the whole, dried pods of the vanilla orchid. If a recipe calls for blending and you have a high-performance blender, simply add the whole bean to the recipe and process it with the other ingredients. Otherwise, split the vanilla bean in half, scrape out the pulp and seeds with a spoon, and discard the outer pod.

YACON SYRUP. Yacon syrup is a sweetener made from the yacon root, a relative of the sunflower. It has a thick, rich brown color, similar to molasses. Yacon syrup is a low-glycemic sweetener, which means it will not rapidly elevate blood sugar.

ZEST. Zest is the colored outer skin layer of citrus fruit. It can be removed with the aid of a citrus zester, vegetable peeler, ultrafine grater, or sharp paring knife. Be careful to use the colored portion only, as the white pith is bitter.

ZUCCHINI. Known as courgette in some parts of the world, zucchini is a long, thin, cylindrical squash with dark to light green skin and firm, off-white flesh. It is plentiful in the summer, both in stores and gardens, though it is typically available year-round in supermarkets. Zucchini range from very small (finger length) to enormous, although the average is about four to eight inches long and two inches in diameter, which is the best size to use when making "spaghetti" or "noodles."

RESOURCES

The following international retailers provide everything you need to stock your kitchen and pantry with raw food staples, seasonings, appliances, and other useful products. Some companies offer both raw and cooked foods, so be sure to specify that you want only raw. Several of these online retailers also offer raw food classes and newsletters, and some have stores where you can shop in person. Visit their websites for a complete listing of their products, services, and contact information.

Australia

Raw Pleasure
www.Raw-Pleasure.com.au   800.729.838

Raw Pleasure is Australia's largest raw food community and source for raw food equipment, events, and superfoods. They carry Excalibur dehydrators, high-powered blenders, juicers, spiral slicers, raw chocolate, crackers, and other raw foods, as well as a wide selection of books on health and nutrition.

Canada

Living Libations
www.LivingLibations.com   416.920.8471 or 705.935.0088

Living Libations offers a wide range of raw chocolate and plant-based body products.

Nujima Living Foods
www.nujima.com   416.761.5111

Nujima Living Foods provides raw, gluten-free, low-glycemic, wild, and organic superfoods from local growers and exotic regions.

TerraTree
www.TerraTree.com   416.654.5357

TerraTree specializes in ready-to-eat live foods including sprouted crackers, pizza bases, flatbreads, savory spreads, and savory dehydrated nuts. All products are made from soaked or sprouted nuts, seeds, and whole grains.

Upaya Naturals

www.UpayaNaturals.com   416.617.3096

Upaya Naturals carries organic, raw, vegan food and healthful lifestyle products including kitchen equipment, shower filters, personal care products, books, and DVDs.

United Kingdom

The Fresh Network

www.fresh-network.com   +44 (0) 845.833. 7017

The Fresh Network offers a wide variety of raw food including nuts and seeds, nut and seed butters, dried fruits, dehydrated foods, olives, seasonings, and treats, as well as kitchen equipment, sprouting tools, nut milk bags, personal care products, and more. They sponsor raw food events and publish a quarterly magazine.

United States

Gold Mine Natural Food

www.goldminenaturalfood.com   800.475.3663

Gold Mine Natural Food carries sea vegetables, sea salt, miso, Nama Shoyu, condiments, dried mushrooms, live cultures, cultured vegetables, raw nuts and seeds, and many other products.

The Raw Gourmet

www.rawgourmet.com   888.316.4611

The Raw Gourmet has items for all your raw food kitchen needs including high-powered blenders, juicers, spiral slicers, mandolines, nut milk bags, books, videos, personal care products, and products for the natural home. They offer a free newsletter and online class, as well as virtual and in-person classes.

SunOrganic Farm

www.sunorganicfarm.com   888.269.9888

SunOrganic Farm carries raw nuts and seeds, dried fruit, raw tahini, raw almond butter, dates, olives, oils, carob powder, herbs, spices, sprouting seeds, and many other products.

International

Raw Food Celebrations   www.RawFoodCelebrations.com

Get the extra resources to help you put this book into action! In the Members Only section of this site, you'll find access to all the hints, tips, color photos, and resources we couldn't jam into the book. Get full shopping lists that make every menu a breeze to prepare. Access this private area of the site with your copy of the book in hand and click "Members Only."

The Living Adventure   www.TheLivingAdventure.com

What would happen if you unearthed profound, life-changing strategies from nature that heightened every part of your life, and you applied all of them at the same time? How would these natural, life-enhancing principals affect how you feel, think, eat, move, and sleep? How would they influence where you live and what you do for a living? What surprises would be in store and how would your life evolve? Share the exciting, real-life experiences of Raw Food Celebrations coauthor Sheryl Duruz and her husband, Piers, for their 12-week grand experiment with learning, loving, and exploring nature that has become known as simply The Living Adventure.

ABOUT THE AUTHORS

Sheryl Duruz

www.TheLivingAdventure.com

Sheryl and her husband Piers founded Raw Pleasure, Australia's largest raw food community and supplier of raw food equipment, education, and inspiration, and The Living Adventure, the grand natural lifestyle enhancement experiment seen around the world. They now live in a forest on a magical Canadian lake and share The Living Adventure. Sheryl found natural, nearly effortless lifestyle answers to lifelong junk food addictions and weight problems and loves how she feels on The Living Adventure. She looks forward to meeting you personally soon.

In 2006 Sheryl decided it was important for everyone to have access to a free, helpful guide with recipes for getting started with raw and living food. Coordinating with over 20 authors and harnessing the power of Raw Pleasure's thousands of worldwide community members, the free *Raw Food Starter Guide* was born and quickly read by over 10,000 people from more than 40 nations. Download your copy now at Sheryl and Piers' website: www.TheLivingAdventure.com.

Nomi Shannon

www.rawgourmet.com • nomi@rawgourmet.com • 888-316-4611 (toll free)

Nomi Shannon "went raw" in 1987 and has never looked back. A well-known proponent of natural health and healing, Nomi is the author of the best-selling book *The Raw Gourmet*. A certified Hippocrates Health Educator since 1995, Nomi has broad training in numerous alternative health modalities, although her main focus is on teaching and writing about raw food, from therapeutic to gourmet. As a live food lifestyle coach, Nomi provides counseling, teaching, and consultation services for individuals and groups the world over who wish to improve their health one bite at a time.

Nomi lives with Rocky the Dog in Bonsall, California, surrounded by avocado and citrus trees. She has two children and one grandchild. To learn more about Nomi Shannon and her teaching schedule, both virtual and live, go to www.rawgourmet.com.

INDEX

blender for, 4
dehydrating/dehydrator for, *3*, 3–4
in *Dressing, Sweet Citrus,* 91
food processor for, 4
Fresh Seasonal, 87
juicer for, 4
Kabobs, 50
mandoline for, 4
Platter with Sweet Dips, 59–60
reamers for, 3
as salad surprise, *11*

G

Gelato, Lemon, 25
Goji-Orange Sauce, 60
grapefruit
    in *Juice, Citrus-Cranberry,* 44
    juicer/reamer for, 3
    as surprise, in salads, *11*
Gravy, Mushroom, 75
green peppers, digestive problem
    with, *13*
Green Power juicer, 4
green(s). *See also* salad(s)
    Herb Sauce, 19
    with Lemon-Basil Dressing, 12
    Wilted, 73
Green Star juicer, 4

H

herbs, 69, 71
Herb Sauce, Green, 19

I

ice cream maker, 4
indigestion, 9
Italian menu/recipes, 9–10
    *Cheesecake, Chocolate-Caramel
        Divine,* 24

Gelato, Lemon, 25
Greens with Lemon-Basil Dressing,
    12
Lasagne, Creamy Tomato, 18–23
*Pasta with Pesto and Marinara
    Sauce, Zucchini,* 14–17
salad ideas, *11*
serving ideas, *10*
*Soup, Parsnip-Avocado with
    Dehydrated Pepper Rounds,* 13

J

Japanese Shoyu Dressing, 64
*Japanese Shoyu Dressing, Summer
    Salad with,* 87
juice
    Apple-Cranberry, 44
    Citrus-Cranberry, 44
    juicers for, 3, 4
*Julienned Vegetables with Sweet
    Citrus Dressing,* 91

K

Kabobs, Fruit, 50
K-Tec Champ HP3A Blender, 4

L

Lasagne, Creamy Tomato, 18–23
lemon(s)
    -Basil Dressing, Greens with, 12
    in *Biscotti, Orange-Coconut,* 93
    Cookies, Luscious, 92
    in *Dressing, Sweet Citrus,* 91
    Gelato, 25
    in *Juice, Citrus-Cranberry,* 44
    juicer/reamer for, 3
    in *Noodles, Zucchini,* 22–23
    in *Sauce, White,* 19

V

Vanilla Nut Nog, 43
vegetable(s). *See also* specific types of
    blender for, 4
    dehydrating/dehydrator for, *3,* 3–4
    food processor for, 4
    juicer for, 4
    in *Loaf, Festive,* 77
    mandoline for, 4
    Platter with Savory Dips, 61–64
    as salad surprise, *11*
    spiral slicer/spiralizer for, 5
    with Sweet Citrus Dressing,
        Julienned, 91
Vita-Mix blender, 4

W

Water, Sweet Raisin, 30

weeping, preventing, 14
White Sauce, 19
Wilted Greens, 73

Y

Yam Pie, 80–81

Z

zucchini
    Canapés, 65
    Noodles, 22–23
    in *Noodles, Pad Thai,* 35
    Pasta with Pesto and Marinara
        Sauce, 14–17
    Roll-Ups, 65
    in *Stuffing,* 71

BOOK PUBLISHING COMPANY

since 1974—books that educate, inspire, and empower

To find your favorite vegetarian and soyfood products online, visit:
www.healthy-eating.com

The Raw Gourmet
Nomi Shannon
978-092047-048-0
$24.95

Hippocrates Life Force
Brian R. Clement, PhD
978-1-57067-204-0
$24.95

Raw Food Made Easy
Jennifer Cornebleet
978-1-57067-175-3
$17.95

Living in the Raw Desserts
Rose Lee Calabro
978-1-57067-201-9
$16.95

Raw Revolution Diet
Cherie Soria
Vesanto Melina, MS, RD
and Brenda Davis, RD
978-1-57067-185-2
$19.95

Celebrating Our Raw Nature
Dorit
978-1-57067-208-8
$14.95

Purchase these health titles and cookbooks from your local bookstore
or natural food store, or you can buy them directly from:

Book Publishing Company • P.O. Box 99 • Summertown, TN 38483
1-800-695-2241

Please include $3.95 per book for shipping and handling.